LAD

BY ANDREW WEBBER

Lad.

First published in 2016

All rights reserved.

No part of this publication may be reproduced, stored in a retrieval system, or transmitted in any form or by any means, electronic, mechanical, photocopying, recording or otherwise, without the prior permission from the author.

Text: © Andrew Webber

Cover design: © Spiffing Covers

The events, characters and companies portrayed in this book are fictitious. Any similarity to real persons, living or dead, is coincidental and not intended by the author.

Chapter One

Sophie's eyes are wide with nerves. She stares at the floor. She stares at the table. She stares at her drink. She stares at anything except me. She's terrified I'll notice the deep pools of sadness swilling around beneath the surface. Beneath the brave face she's painted on with layers of MAC make-up.

Her hands run through her long, dark hair. They search for something to do, desperate to keep busy, endlessly twirling the blow-dried ringlets that brush against her shoulders. She picks up her gin and tonic and takes another sip. She'll have drained the whole thing in a couple of minutes if she keeps that up. She tries not to well up when she mentions the ex that broke her heart. The betrayal's obviously still fresh.

"It's just so hard to meet someone you can trust," she says, her dark saucer eyes staring at me for reassurance.

I look her in the eye and put my hand on hers. Sometimes a tiny bit of human contact is all people are looking for. I look her straight in the eye and say, "I know exactly what you mean."

What Sophie's looking for is a *Knight in Shining Armour*. Someone to take care of her. Someone to tell her everything's going to be alright. To show her that not all blokes are the same. That we aren't all cheating shits. Not like the last bastard who ran off with her best friend after a shagging her on the sly for two-years. Sophie's taking her first Bambi steps back into the dating world tonight, with me, in this pub, ten minutes from Clapham station. I make the appropriate noises at the appropriate points. I nod along while she vents about her ex. About how he made her feel. About how he betrayed her trust. She talks about how hard it is to meet people these days. That's where the real fear comes from. The worry that she'll be left on the shelf. She's scared that everyone's paired off and she's missed the boat.

I tell her I know how she feels. That I've been there too. That I know how much it hurts. That all I want is to meet someone and be happy. I confess to her that this is the first time I've plucked up the courage to go out on a date in nearly a year. I'm lying of course. I was in this very bar only two nights ago with someone else. A fat-arsed dullard called Kimberley. We didn't get past the first drink before I cut that short. She was absolutely horrendous.

This is my first date bar; The Duck on Battersea Rise. It's got that warm pub feel, which relaxes people, but it's littered with cosy tables that remind people they're still on a date, not just meeting someone down the pub for a couple of drinks. Obviously if they show promise there are better, more romantic places for a second date.

Kimberley did not show promise.

Sophie does.

She's hurt, vulnerable and totally bereft of confidence. Just the way I like them.

It's all too easy really. I mirror her melancholy and she sees a kindred spirit. Someone who understands. We have a couple more drinks and she starts to relax. We cosy up on the couch. "I've never felt so comfortable with someone so quickly," she says.

"I know what you mean," I say, "I feel like I've known you for years." I snake an arm around her, testing the waters.

She smiles and places her head on my shoulder. We drink more. An alcohol-fuelled fog descends upon us. A red-wine grin stretches across her face. "I don't want this night to end," she says.

I need to play this just right now. Come on too strong and she'll be spooked, not strong enough and the night will fade away into a couple of hours of pointless kissing and cuddling. "Me too," I say. "If we'd known each other longer I'd invite you back with me. Just to keep talking and getting to know each other. I feel like we've still got so much to say."

It hits the target. "Really?" she looks up at me, eyes wide, betraying her excitement.

"Really," I say. "I just feel so comfortable being around you. I feel like you really understand who I am." I pause for a second. "I just don't want to rush into anything you know?"

"It's ok," she says, kissing me gently on the cheek, "I trust you."

She shyly links her fingers through mine on the short walk back to my flat. The other reason I always choose The Duck is it's only a ten minute walk home. It's good planning in case the date goes as well as this. Occasionally this will happen organically, like with Sophie. She wanted to come back, I just had to ask her the right way. Others are a bit more sceptical. For those ones I pretend there's an emergency back at the flat. If they come with me then I know I'm onto a winner. If not, well then at least I'm out of there before I waste too much time on them.

We get back to mine, and I open the bottle of wine I'd put in the fridge, just in case. Pinot Grigio. Every girl likes Pinot. It's a safe bet. I can hear my flatmate locked away in his room, listening to his depressing music. Nineties grunge played by people who can't get over their exes. Listened to by people who can't get over their exes.

"Oh I like that song," Sophie says as she hears the downbeat melody waft into the living room. Of course she does.

We go through the charade of choosing a movie. I pick 'Along Came Polly', with Ben Stiller and Jennifer Aniston. It's pointless as our hands are all over each before the opening credits have even finished. I've got one hand up her top and another working on her belt when she asks to move into the bedroom. She's too shy to continue on the sofa in case my flatmate comes out of his misery-den. No chance of that, he's probably in there slitting his wrists as we speak, but I'm all about making the girl feel comfortable, so we head behind the safety of my bedroom door and I make short work of that belt.

The best thing about girls like Sophie, apart from how easy it is to convince them to come home with me, is the sex. They think they're getting back at the guy who hurt them by sleeping with me. They release all that anger as they exorcise the demons of the previous relationship. Taking that first step and moving on with another guy is a kind of catharsis for them. They never fail to enjoy it. All that repressed desire is unleashed. You can get away with all sorts. You can almost see them awaken to the idea that there is life outside of their old shitty relationship. A better life away from the same old selfish lump mauling them during the ad breaks of X-Factor. It's quite an experience. For both of us.

The catharsis of the previous night is forgotten in the morning, as the banshee of the early hours clambers back into her shell. She feels some guilt of course. They always do. She makes the same awkward confession they all make. That she's never done anything like that before. That she really hopes I don't think less of her because of it. "Of course not," I say. "I've never done anything like that before either."

She's dubious, to her credit. Normally they lap that line straight up. "Honestly," I say, "I wouldn't just invite someone back who I hadn't fallen for."

Sophie melts, reassured that I feel just like she does. That I've found someone I've got a real connection with. She sits on the end of the bed, shyly collecting her clothes from the floor and pulling her top back over her head, as if covering herself up will mean she regains some modesty. As if her naked body writhing beneath me isn't forever burnt into my memory and stored for future reference.

I walk her to the front door and kiss her on the lips, a tender goodbye that further reassures her that I'm not the same as the others. That I'm one of the good guys. She lingers, wanting to stay. "I'll call you later," I whisper, holding her hand until the last possible moment as she turns to walk down the communal corridor and back out into the elements. I wait at the door and give her a little smile as she turns around one more time, aching for that final confirmation before she disappears. I close the door after she leaves.

I'm not going to call her later.

She's got clingy written all over her.

Chapter Two

The phone on my desk rings. I pick it up and trot out the necessary greeting, "Barrie and Aberdeen, you're through to the sales desk." The words, like everything else here, emerge of their own accord. No brain power required. A hesitant voice answers me. An old lady by the sound of it.

"I wonder if you can help me," she stutters, "I need to sell my house."

"That's great," I say, politely as always, "I can certainly help you with that. Why don't you give me some details?"

"My husband's just passed away you see," she says. It must be recent, her voice still trembles when she airs the words. As if speaking them makes it real.

"I'm terribly sorry to hear that," I reply. I pride myself on my impeccable manners in the workplace.

"It's just Harold used to deal with all of the finances. It's all a bit of a mess. I'm a bit worried about all the bills. I think maybe selling the house might be the best course of action. You know, to get everything squared away. Draw a line under things."

Bingo. I finger the keys on my mobile as I send a text to Nick, to let him know I may have a potential lead, as I tell her I understand perfectly and I know how difficult these things are. That I'll be more than willing to drop round for a cup of tea if it makes her feel better so that she can give me some more information. Nick texts back immediately. He's in the market. I need to let him know once I've found out more. When I know it's a goer.

I head over to see the old dear's place straight away. My phone buzzes. It's Sophie. She wants to say thanks for a lovely night, and asks what I'm doing on Thursday? I ignore it. Sophie needs to chill out. I mean, she only left my place three hours ago and she's already on my case.

The old biddy's place is an absolute goldmine. Four beds, two baths, two receptions, conservatory and a bloody great garden. It needs a bit of modernising, obviously. Fuck knows why old people are so obsessed with floral wallpaper, green bathtubs and shaggy carpet. But it's worth eight hundred at least. Maybe a bit more if the market picks up towards the summer. I need to play this right.

We sit down for a cup of tea, opposite each other on two small sofas that must be thirty years old if they're a day. I crowbar as much information from her as possible. It's easy as it's just me and her. There are no meddling kids sticking their noses in, protecting their inheritance under the guise of supporting their mum through a difficult time. She can't remember how long they've lived there. A good sign. Her husband, Harold, she still says his name wistfully while she looks upwards, passed away about a month ago. She mentions all the bills coming through the front door. I chance my arm.

"I reckon we could get you about six-hundred and fifty thousand, perhaps a little bit less if you're in a hurry to sell, Mrs O'Shea."

She looks shocked. For a second I think I've blown it. "Oh my word," she says, "that would be amazing."

Jackpot.

"I'll speak to one of my investors," I say, "they're always on the lookout for beautiful houses like this."

Her face clouds over slightly. "I don't want to sell it to anyone who's going to rent it out to loads of people. This was our home. Harold and I lived here for our whole married life. It means a lot to me. I want to pass it on to someone who'll treat it the same way."

"Of course." I reply, full in the knowledge that Nick will have this place cut up into five bedrooms and rented out to about ten people within a month of buying it, "Let me get back to the office and speak to a few people. I'll give you a call later on if that's ok with you?"

She calls me young man and thanks me profusely when I leave. She's practically teary-eyed. I call Nick on the way back to the office. Nick is big time. He's got property worth tens of millions all over the country. He's got a few people like me on his payroll. Spotters he calls us. Some estate agents like me, a few divorce lawyers and a couple of probate solicitors. If a deal like this comes up he gets the call first, before it even goes on the market. He needs at least twenty percent discount off the market price for it to be worth his while. Then he can use one of his fancy buy-and-re-mortgage tricks, meaning he ends up with a massive house without putting any of his own money into it. Genius really. He bungs me a few grand when I find him a deal. It's a win-win. The key is finding someone looking to sell quickly. Nick calls them *distressed sellers*. Says he's an expert in *leveraging people's time pressure*. He's even got a funeral home that gives out his card as part of their package.

I need this as well. Not just the cash, but I need the sale to get ahead of Charlie in the yearly sales leaderboard. There's not long left and if I can win that it'll be another five grand bonus. I tell Nick the details. He's keen. He's going to drive up from Brighton this afternoon to check the place out and gauge how far we can push the old crow.

I'm back in the office typing up the details as soon as I can to send Nick via email. He likes to do his homework when he's going to meet a potential seller. I send them across just before one and grab my keys, ready to bolt out the door for a quick lunch. Subway. Italian BMT. Footlong. I notice Sophie's messaged me again, to check if I got her earlier text. I delete the message and block her number. Birds like her do my head in.

It's just before three when Nick pulls up in his Range Rover sport. I'm waiting outside the old lady's front gate for him, so we can present a united front. Everything about him screams success. His car. His Italian tailored suit. The way he shakes your hand. He's wearing Ray-bans today as well, which is a bit unnecessary, what with it only being the first week in February. They make him look like some kind of middle-aged Miami Vice tribute act. I don't mention that of course. I made fifteen grand off him last year. I'm not jeopardising that. Without that cash I'd still be driving around in a Vauxhall Nova, not the gleaming Audi TT parked back at home. The bosses won't let me use it at work. They say it gives people the wrong impression. Makes them think we're making too much money. Totally the wrong attitude in my book. Just look at Nick. People want to work with him *because* he looks successful.

We go inside and Nick's as charming as a new boyfriend meeting the parents for the first time. He even gives her a hug when he tells her how sorry he is about old Harold. He's remembered the old stiff's name of course. A real touch of class.

"You've such a beautiful house here Mrs O'Shea," he begins.

She interrupts him; "Please, call me Maggie my dear." She's putty already.

"It'd be my pleasure Maggie," he says accentuating the Maggie pleasantly. "I understand you are looking to move quite quickly?"

She hesitates. "Well, I don't have anywhere else to go, but I'm just so worried about these bills." She gestures at what's already a sizeable stack on her coffee table. Council tax and utility companies are all total shits in this kind of situation. They were probably hounding her while the old boy's body was still warm. It's terrible but it doesn't half make it easier for the likes of Nick.

"I totally understand," says Nick, putting his hand gently on her arm, "you know, we might be able to come to some kind of arrangement. What about if I bought the house from you, which solves the problem of all these bills, but then I let you stay here as long as you want? That way you can take your time and find somewhere else to move to when you're good and ready?"

She practically jumps on him. "Oh that would be wonderful. A real load off my mind."

"I tell you what then," he says, smelling blood in the water, "I'll get Danny here to organise a survey as soon as possible. As soon as we've got that, we'll come to an agreement over a nice cup of tea and get all this mess sorted out for you."

"You're a pair of angels," she says as she clutches us by the front door on the way out. It's enough to make you go all misty-eyed. We walk to the car in silence, as if we're scared to utter a word out loud in case we get rumbled.

"Bite to eat?" suggests Nick. He wants to talk tactics.

"Sure," I say with one eye on the time. It's already after four and Speed Dating starts at seven. Ideally I'd like to fit in a sunbed beforehand. We head to a little pub about fifteen minutes away, where the suburbs begin to drift into the countryside. It's a clandestine operation, wholly unnecessary, but I think it makes Nick feel more important so I roll with it.

"How much did you tell her it was worth?" asks Nick, cutting straight to the chase as soon as he's ordered us a couple of steak sandwiches.

"Six-fifty."

"And it's worth what? Eight? Maybe Eight-fifty?"

"Eight-fifty with a bit of work."

"Ok," he says, sitting back in his chair. I can see the cogs turning.

"Can you get your mate to do the survey?" He throws the question out nonchalantly, as if he hasn't just asked me to commit fraud.

"No problem," I reply.

"It needs to be valued at six-fifty."

I nod. If you're going to make it up it doesn't really matter what the value needs to be. "Same deal?" I ask.

"Five hundred for your mate to do the survey. Three grand for you when the deal goes through."

I nod again. In my head I'm already throwing twenties at strippers down Secrets in Hammersmith. Our steak sandwiches arrive. We eat them in silence, both of our minds counting the money in the pipeline.

Chapter Three

You're normally lucky if one in five is doable at a speed dating night, but the hulking monstrosity sat opposite me is a new low even by those piss-poor standards. It's actually ridiculous. I'm barely able to stop myself from laughing in her face as I sit down. I half expect Jeremy Beadle to jump out pissing himself until I remember he can't. He's dead.

"Do you like milk?" she says, before I've even got myself sat down properly. There's a half finished pint of semi-skimmed in front of her, most of which she seems to have smeared around her lips in some sort of thick paste. The rest appears to have made its way down the front of her t-shirt, which judging from its colour and size was bought an awful long time ago, when she was half the age and weight. The translucent stain covers the E and A, but I can tell by the faded killer whale it's from Sea World. I idly wonder if she has a carer waiting for her in the bar area.

"It's ok I suppose," I reply. It's not something I've ever really considered.

An awkward silence fills the air, which she breaks by sighing and taking another slurp. Clearly she was hoping for a bit more enthusiasm. She slowly wipes her hand across her face, inadvertently increasing the milk coverage across her chin and cheeks. I don't say anything. I glance at the clock above her head. This is going to be a long five minutes.

"How about flavoured milk?" she asks.

She's clutching at straws, but I appreciate the effort she's making to get the conversation going. I sure as hell don't want to sit here for the entire five minutes while she silently seethes at me, so I consider my response to this one a bit more carefully. I answer in the positive. She relaxes. A healthy debate ensues around the relative pros and cons of Nesquik (stronger flavour, long brand history but pricey and only available in cartons) compared with Yazoo (cheaper and bottle-based but a weaker strawberry flavour, which she feels is the benchmark for the brand's overall quality). With this established, the conversation dries up once again. I glance at the clock. A minute remains. She stares blankly at me. I reach down into the depths of my mind to come up with something to fill the last remaining moments of silence.

"Where does Frijj fit into this whole landscape?" I say, and immediately realise from the expression slapped all over her face that I've made a massive faux-pas.

"That's a milkshake. Not a flavoured milk," she replies sullenly. The smile disappears from her face and all goodwill I've accumulated over the past four minutes vanishes down the drain. She looks at me with contempt and excuses herself to find the bathroom, clearly having heard enough. I stare blankly at her glass of milk then watch the clock tick down the last eight seconds.

Speed dating is a regular event at The Grove, a bar about twenty minutes away from my flat. It's one of those places that used to be a pub before it had a slight refurb, replaced the fish and chips with corn-fed chicken on a bed of quinoa, doubled the drinks prices and called itself a Gastropub. The old crowd all baulked at the idea of paying a fiver for a pint and disappeared to another pub. Their places are now taken by a younger clientele, all fake tan and hairspray. And that's just the blokes. The place is a real hotspot for the bright young things of the area. I try to get down here at least once every couple of weeks and I never miss a speed dating night.

The buzzer sounds and I move along to my next date. She is utterly non-descript. The very definition of average. Mousey brown hair. No tits to speak of. Pale skin. Neither skinny, athletic or fat. Just totally pointless. A nothing. She introduces herself. I forget her name instantly. She's from some town in the middle of some county I've never heard of, probably near Birmingham or Derby or some other dive. The sort of place where the village phone box is somewhere to hang out. No doubt they all huddled around it, even in the winter, drinking cans of cider before heading to the nearest field to push over some cows or something. She came to London a couple of years ago for a bit of excitement. She works in accounts. She wouldn't know excitement if it dipped its knob in her drink. Our five minutes pass and I already have no recollection of our conversation.

A broad Welsh twang greets me at the next table. A cute brunette named Natalie with a girl-next-door type charm to her. She spends the next five minutes sweetly explaining a series of horrific things she's done to people around her. Including cutting contact with her poverty-stricken family back in a deprived north Welsh mining town two years ago. Apparently their lack of money was embarrassing for a high-flying city exec like her. She laughs as she tells me about sleeping with her flatmate's boyfriend while she was asleep in the room next door; and robotically explains that she dumped her boyfriend a month ago, the day before his father's funeral, because his unhappiness was stressing her out. She is clearly a psychopath. She is also, however, vaguely attractive, so I give her my number. The crazy ones are always great in the sack.

A succession of pointless girls fills the next five timeslots, before finally, I reach the one I've been waiting for the entire night; a particularly stunning bottle-blonde. She's fake-tanned to within an inch of her life and her toned body is crammed into a dress at least three sizes too small for her, with a plunging neckline which shows off her gravity-defying tits. Probably fake. The entire room has been gawping at her the whole night so far. I've already given her the eye a bit and I can tell she's keen. I sit down. "Hello you," she purrs, and

I know it's a done deal. She is the very embodiment of why I never miss speed dating at The Grove.

She's chatty and doesn't shut up for the entire five minutes. I can barely get a word in edgeways, which I don't mind, as I spend the allotted time looking down her cleavage and nodding along to the relentless stream of consciousness making its way from her pea-sized brain through her botoxed lips. The buzzer goes. We hold each other's gaze and exchange a smile. "I'll wait for you at the end," I say, as I stand up. She is absolutely made up.

I don't bother with the final two dates, who are both total munters anyway, and head straight to a table on the far side of the bar, away from the speed dating free for all. A doable waitress brings me a pint over. She's a seven. Great arse, average face. The blonde takes my lead and within a few minutes she's marched straight over to join me at my carefully selected table for two in the corner.

"So are you going to buy me a drink then?" she says. Her eyes glitter with intent.

"Of course," I say, motioning to the waitress to come over.

"There's just one slight complication," she says, touching my arm and smiling sweetly. Here we go. She's going to tell me she's got a cock or something.

"My best mate's with me, and she'll go mad if I ditch her for some bloke I've only just met. Do you mind if she joins us?" She leans in as she asks, showing as much cleavage as possible. I get the impression she's used that tactic before. It works, obviously. Her mate might even be fit and up for it as well. Double trouble. "She's so quirky" she says. "You'll love her. She's absolutely hilarious. And don't worry, I promise I'll make it worth your while."

"Oh go on then," I answer in mock defeat.

"Great," says the blonde, "I'll just go and grab her. She's just at the bar getting herself a glass of milk."

Oh for fuck's sake.

Chapter Four

Chris moved in with me about three months ago and seems to exist in a constant state of existential crisis. He hates his job, working for a gas company somewhere out in the murky depths of Middlesex, but can't seem to bring himself to leave. He just goes through the motions with the resignation of someone who's too scared to make a change.

He spends the rest of his life in the flat, ninety percent of which he's holed up in his bedroom listening to endless loops of bitter, heartbroken grunge music or some dreadful wailing shite like Radiohead, which probably only serves to magnify the feeling that his life is utterly pointless and without hope. Which I suppose it is.

His ex-girlfriend Anna, who it has to be said, was fit, finally realised she was much better than him about three months ago and chucked him for a moronic Saffer called Todd, whose only memorable features seemed to be a smattering of tribal tattoos, long hair and a barely concealed tendency for racism.

Chris hasn't taken it brilliantly, and about the only time he does emerge from his room, it's generally to stuff takeaway pizza down his throat while he watches appallingly geeky films, like Lord of the Rings or Star Wars. The sort of thing you'd rightly be bullied for when you were at school. I know this because we went to the same school, and while I never *technically* bullied him, I did find his ordeal pretty hilarious for most of my teenage years.

Miserable music, shite films, takeaway food and a job he hates. If I ever get to that stage I'd like to think I'd do the honourable thing and jump off the nearest tall building. But then, if he did, I wonder if anyone would really notice. I'm a big believer in a man being self-sufficient. I like to spend time on my own, but I always keep people around for when I want them. But Chris is properly alone. He's literally got no one.

He's really let himself go since he moved in as well. All that pizza hasn't done him any favours. His belly's expanding at a rate of knots, he hasn't shaved for about two months now, and his hair is a lanky, greasy mess. I noticed he'd bought a load of baggy clothes from TK Maxx last week as well. Another sign of a man who's given up on life.

I take great enjoyment in hammering home the miserable solitude of his existence as often as possible by ensuring my attempts to knob my way around Clapham's female population are loud enough to wake the dead, let alone my thirty-three year old loser flatmate who weeps himself to sleep every night wondering where it all went wrong. Speed Date Jennie, or Julie, or whatever the fuck her name is, turns out to be an excellent collaborator, and wails like a demented demon as I relentlessly pump her around the room until the early hours. I even make sure to do her up against the wall between Chris's room and mine. Just to really make sure he hears how a real lad gets the job done. I had to sit and listen to her and her milk-freak mate until closing time at The Grove but by god it was worth it. The filth coming out of her mouth is exceptional. Real below the counter stuff. I make a mental note to get her phone number as she breathlessly begs me to slap her red-raw arse-cheeks for what must be the fiftieth time.

We finally take a breather around three-thirty. She's panting like Pavarotti doing the marathon and her legs are still shaking a good five minutes after I've rolled off her. There's that awkward silence you get after you've fucked someone you don't know very well and realise you have absolutely no idea what to talk to them about. I plump for, "I'll call you a cab," which doesn't go down brilliantly.

I've never been able to get my head around the female obsession with staying over. I don't know this girl at all. *At all.* She could be a total nut-job. A complete bunny-boiler. Or worse still she might snore. Why the fuck would I want her dribbling on my shoulder all night anyway? I'm a light sleeper at the best of times, if she keeps me awake all night doing her best Homer Simpson impression the chances of us meeting up again are non-existent. She doesn't realise I'm doing her a favour and flounces around in a strop for a few moments. Her performance finally ends when I chuck my phone onto the bed and tell her to put her number in. She types her name, which actually turns out to be Michelle, followed by her mobile number, work number and email address. She's really covered all the bases there. It's safe to say she's up for another session, even if I am kicking her out in the middle of the night.

I do the gentlemanly thing and walk her to the door when the cab arrives, giving her behind, which is now back in its original skin-tight packaging, a final playful slap. She presses against me by the door, and for a minute I think she's going to start up again there and then, but sadly not. She looks back and waves a few times on her way to the front door of the building but I close the door after the third. It's nearly four in the morning on a Wednesday night and I can't be arsed with all this soppy bollocks.

I open up the window when I get back into my room to air out the lingering hum of three hours of drunken shagging. A breeze creeps in and brushes away the thin layer of sweat still hugging me. There's nothing more relaxing than the post-shag moment of silence. Especially when I've managed to send the bird home straight afterwards.

I close my eyes for a second and remember the terrible insomnia I used to suffer from a few years ago. Back when life wasn't all fun and games. I used to sit there staring at the ceiling all night. I tried everything; Herbal tablets. Over the counter pills. Prescription drugs.

Rescue Remedy. Lavender under the pillow. Nothing worked. It turns out the best medicine is a marathon session of filth with a random girl. Different remedies for different people I guess. I know what works for me and I try to take it as often as possible.

Chapter Five

Friday mornings are dull affairs. Our manager David makes a big song and dance about the weekly sales update. Charlie's smug at the moment as he's got his nose in front, but if all goes to plan over the next couple of weeks I'll get Nick sale agreed on Mrs O'Shea's place and I'll be miles ahead by the end of the financial year. That end of year bonus is as good as mine.

Charlie specialises in flogging piddly little one and two bed flats. To be fair to him he's pretty good at it, but he'll need to sell about five more to overtake me again once the old dear's house goes through. He's got no chance. Still, got to let him have his moment in the sun. He beams at everyone as David runs through the leaderboard.

The whole place is a joke really. Me and Charlie are the only ones worth our wages in the entire place. Everyone else is miles behind. Alice, who I'd politely describe as dim-witted, is a distant third. Her questionable ability to string a sentence together being her main liability. She's borderline attractive, making up for her exceptionally plain features with an enormous rack. She's a five. Maybe a six after a few beers. Charlie maintains that she's a seven, but that's just because he shagged her at the Christmas do. I noticed they'd both disappeared towards the end of the night and caught them at it behind the pub. I took a picture on my phone and put them up all over the office the next day. Absolutely classic banter. Alice didn't see the funny side though and burst out crying. I had to see David about it the next day. The prick gave me a verbal warning. That's the problem with everyone these days. No one's got a sense of humour anymore. The silly bint still doesn't talk to me and that was about two months ago.

Colin's bringing up the rear on the sales leaderboard with only eight sales all year. I honestly don't know how he keeps a roof over his head. He's the sort of bloke who looks untidy wearing a tuxedo. He's got one creased suit, which I'm pretty sure he never washes. He wears crinkled grey shirts underneath, that I'm sure started life some years before classed as white. He washes his hair about as often as his suit and he has the faint stink of someone who only showers every couple of days. That kind of musty smell you normally only find around old people on the bus. No wonder he never makes any sales. Anyone being shown round a house by him probably thinks the place has got a sewage problem. Despite never making any sales, he's been working at Barrie and Aberdeen for ten years. He's David's brother.

Our manager David is the kind of dickhead who follows every rule in the book. If there isn't a rule, he'll sure as hell make one up, which is probably why he's forty-five and earning eighteen grand a year. He wears colourful ties depending on which day of the week it is, apart from Christmas, when he breaks out his traditional flashing Rudolf monstrosity. He's always trying to organise team nights out but even Alice makes an excuse not to go. David's got it in for me, always sticking his nose in, checking all my paperwork, just to make sure I've followed the correct procedure. Needless to say, he's got zero banter.

I spend the rest of the morning being talked at by a pair of first-time buyers. A pointless exercise in every respect. They haven't got a deposit and stand absolutely no chance of getting a mortgage above two hundred grand. They insist on seeing the details of every house and flat we have on the market.

"Oooh I like this one," says Jo-Jo the part time barista, pointing at a five-hundred grand house with an enormous garden and off-street parking. I want to throttle her. My frustration only heightens when a middle-aged couple looking to buy their daughter a flat stroll into the office and straight up to Charlie's desk. He prints off six lots of property details, all of which they're interested in. They want to buy in cash. I quietly seethe as Jo-Jo waxes lyrical about the house she grew up in, the carefree summers in the garden and her mother's flair in the kitchen. Her boyfriend Marcus seems to read my mind and cuts the conversation short. I somehow manage to smile and shake them both by the hand as they exit with a stack of print-outs, none of which they can afford. Charlie smugly grins at me after they've gone. I tell him to fuck off.

Friday lunchtimes down the Bird and Bison have become something of a tradition for me and Charlie. We order a couple of pints of Kronenburg and I pull out a little red notebook while we wait for our regular food order to appear. He has the burger, I have the fish. The notebook contains a week by week tally of the number of girls we've each slept with so far this year. Each week has a column for new conquests, and a cumulative total for the year to date. Needless to say I am wiping the floor with him.

"So?" he asks.

"Two more."

He sighs, "Who?"

"Sophie on Tuesday night." He grimaces. That's a sore one for him. We'd both been messaging her online over the last few weeks, but I managed to pin her down for a date first. He had been still trying to get one organised but now there was no point. "And some girl from the speed dating on Wednesday night, who was an absolute belter in the sack. Total filth. How about yourself?" I ask with a grin. I already know the answer. It's always obvious when Charlie's got lucky. He comes in crowing about it the moment he next walks into the office. That hadn't happened for a few weeks now.

"None," he sighs. He hesitates before sheepishly adding, "Unless you let me count Alice again?"

"You didn't?" I say.

He nods. "Monday after work. I was helping her with a sale at the end of the day and we went for a quick drink after. One thing led to another." We laugh. I give him a high-five which he reluctantly accepts. Fair play to him. Any port in a storm and all that. I total up the cumulative. I'm on twenty-five for the year. Only a few weeks left. Not a bad average.

Charlie's on eleven. A poor return for someone of his calibre. He used to be a machine but he's lost his touch ever since he had an accident on his bike about eighteen months ago. He had a load of trouble around the same time when his ex-girlfriend found out he'd been trying to knob her best mate. Since then he's being showing troubling signs of some kind of conscience. Pathetic really. He's also started to make noises about not wanting to continue with our little competition as well. Keeps saying it's immature. He's just gutted he's so far behind. I remind him there's two hundred quid riding on it.

We fit another pint in, as it's a Friday. We both need them to get through a mind-numbing afternoon at Barrie and Aberdeen. We sink them sharpish and head back to the office. David's out with a potential seller, sizing up their property. He's still none the wiser about Mrs O'Shea's gaff. I need to keep that off his radar until the sale's agreed. Colin's out on his lunch break, probably reading his book in the park like the loser that he is. It's just me, Charlie and Alice. I can't resist piping up.

"Oi Oi," I shout across the silence in the direction of Alice, "I hear you and Charlie had another couple of rounds on Monday night."

She glances at Charlie for a moment, mouth hanging open. Then runs out of the front door crying. For fuck's sake. It was only a bit of banter.

Chapter Six

Amy is the only girl in the last five years to have infiltrated my Friday nights. Occasionally, and only if I've got no plans with the lads, I even let her come over on a Saturday. Truth be told, I'm not entirely sure how she's managed it. We first met about a year ago. A classic Tuesday night first date. She walked into a non-descript pub in Putney with a massive grin plastered across her face. I now suspect the wind changed when she was a little girl and she's been stuck with that expression ever since, as I'm pretty sure I've only ever seen her deliriously happy.

She made me laugh straight away, which was strange, as I don't even like female comedians normally, let alone standard birds. I just don't find jokes about being fat and having periods funny. But Amy had banter. Proper lad banter. A rare find.

After a couple of hours I realised I hadn't spent the entire evening scheming to get her into bed. Or down an alley. Or even just into the pub toilets. About half the time, but not the entire evening, which was unusual. I'd actually been listening to her. By the time she'd pulled me into a perfectly placed darkened corner on the way to the bus stop for a snog I'd already promoted her to a Thursday night second date slot.

My admission to Charlie the next morning that I was upgrading her without actually getting any action first caused a raised eyebrow and an accusation that I was going soft. I refuted that suggestion by nailing the work-experience girl later that night. I forget her name. Thursdays weren't agreeable to Amy though, and before I'd really noticed, she'd elbowed her way into my sacred weekends. I don't remember if it was ever really discussed but for some reason I didn't object. It's been that way ever since. It turns out that watching a movie with Amy on a Friday night after five straight days of office bullshit at Barrie and Aberdeen is a decent way to end the week.

Amy arrives at six-thirty on the dot, as always. She dumps her overnight bag in my room and we head straight out to Nando's. She grins at me as she interlinks her fingers with mine on the stroll down there. I don't normally go in for public displays of affection but I allow Amy this concession. Starting off the evening with her getting in a mood because I won't hold her hand would not be a smart move. She swings our linked hands like a hyperactive child. She's excited for Fridays, and Nando's and movie night at my place. But then, Amy's excited about pretty much everything in life. It's this relentless enthusiasm, her yin to my cynical yang, that's enabled her to bounce into my life with total disregard for my weekly routine.

We stand in a queue behind a group of twelve teenagers. Of course, they all have to order and count out their pocket money separately. This infuriates me to the point of violence, but Amy simply laughs it off. Finally, we make it through the horde to our regular server, Pieter, whose face brightens at the sight of customers who aren't fifteen and paying in coins.

"Hi guys," he practically bursts, "the usual?"

"Yes please Pieter," she bursts back, "and don't forget the Perinaise." She high-fives him when we complete the transaction. She sings a song from Frozen as we wait for our food, which delights the two children next to us who are convinced she is some kind of princess. Their dad and I exchange rolled eyes.

As always, we stop off at the off-license on the way home. I clutch the bag of warm food as she charges into the store. The owner greets her like a long lost friend. She comes round once a week and knows everyone. I, the local resident of five years, hover in the background, invisible. We exit after another high-five, a bottle of

Pinot Grigio and a giant bag of chocolate buttons added to our regular haul.

We return to the flat and find Chris already bunkered down on the sofa, awaiting his pizza delivery, Jurassic Park paused at the opening credits. He's waiting for us before starting his evening's entertainment, under the guise of waiting for his pizza. "I love Jurassic Park," Amy squeals as she greets him with another high-five. They get on like a house on fire, and I immediately realise that much of my evening is going to be spent watching a bloody dinosaur movie with Chris, not humping Amy like a rabbit on heat, which disappoints me.

"How are you feeling about everything?" she asks Chris.

I brace myself for the re-telling of the story I've heard about six thousand times over the last few months about his ex, Anna, and how she left him for Todd, and about how unfair it is, but he simply smiles at Amy and answers, "Fine, thanks". I try not to stare at him open-mouthed. Maybe he's finally turned the corner. I mean, he is still spending Friday night on his own, watching Jurassic Park and scoffing pizza but still, baby steps.

We watch Jurassic Park until the bitter end. Amy's oblivious to how antsy I'm getting as she whoops and hollers her way through the film with Chris, laughing when she remembers what a minor role Samuel L Jackson has and screaming from behind her hands when the Velociraptors stalk the children in the kitchen. By the time the Tyrannosaur is roaring at the end of the film I am ready to do the same. As soon as the end credits roll I stand, hinting in no uncertain terms that it is time to head to the bedroom. That is, after all, the main point of her even being here. She follows a couple of minutes behind me, having said goodnight to her movie buddy Chris.

"Is somebody in a bad mood?" she teases as she enters my room. I ignore her. She continues regardless. "Is somebody not getting enough attention tonight?"

I try manfully to maintain my annoyance at having to sit through the entire film while she and Chris acted like I wasn't there, but there's something about Amy that makes it impossible to be mad with her.

"Do you want me to make it up to you?" she coos. That does it. I smile at her and all is forgiven. I allow her to make it up to me. Which she does. Emphatically. A few times. I normally like to be in charge but there's no arguing with Amy when she's in this sort of mood.

A couple of hours later, she's completely spent. She snuggles in, still breathing heavily from the exertion. I put my arm around her. Again, I don't really like that sort of thing but she's earned it. She's asleep within a few moments, gently snoring about an inch from my face. Normally snoring disgusts me but I can't help but find everything she does hilarious. It doesn't bother me that much and within a few minutes I'm out too. I wake up around three to find Amy hasn't, in fact, spent all her energy. Nor has she finished making everything up to me. Sensational. What a top girl she is.

We stay in bed until just after nine the next morning, chatting bollocks. We have one last session before she heads off to some run she's doing with a group of mates, which is ideal as she's out of the flat by the time my alarm goes off at half-nine, and I'm up for my first coffee and protein shake of the day, before the customary big sesh down the gym with Gaz and Charlie.

Chapter Seven

The punishments for missing the meet time on a boys' night are heavy. One downed pint for every five minutes you're late. About three months ago Ritz had to do five pints in a row after he turned up half an hour after the rest of us. Admittedly his brother had been in a car crash, but rules are rules. He puked halfway through the drinks but managed to finish the lot. Fair play to him. Unfortunately he passed out in the corner of the pub at eight-thirty and proceeded to wet himself about ten minutes later, in full view of the rest of the pub. We drew a cock on his head and moved on. Classic banter.

Since then no one's been late for a night out.

The rest of the Wolf Pack, as we like to call ourselves, is made up of Gaz, Charlie and Ben.

Gaz is wearing some kind of pale blue cotton abomination tonight, a good couple of sizes too small for him, stretched mercilessly across his hulking shoulders. It makes him look like a giant smurf. His dress sense is absolutely appalling. It's a bit of a running joke amongst the rest of the lads. He shaves his head close to the scalp, which only serves to emphasise the colossal pair of ears jutting out from the side of his head. I swear he can probably pick up Radio One with them. It normally takes Gaz at least a second longer than everyone else to get a joke which is all the more noticeable because of his braying laugh. It makes him sound like a donkey watching comic relief. I think he may be on some kind of spectrum.

Sadly for Gaz he's never been much of a hit with the ladies. He does, however, possess awareness of this fact, and will no doubt patiently wait for the end of the night tonight, as always, whereupon he'll begin minesweeping the dancefloor for any stragglers old and pissed enough to entertain going home with him. It's a strategy that has given him some decent results. And some real shockers. About six months ago he pulled an old bird whose tits were so saggy I swear she could have charged the bar for cleaning the floor while she was dancing.

Ben is always the first one to bring up some of Gaz's more questionable conquests. Ben's a piss-taking shaven-headed mockney with expensive clothes and a relentless sex addiction. There's no situation too inappropriate for Ben to try and get into someone's knickers. He's always lived by the motto that if you don't buy a ticket you don't win the lottery. He sells sporting memorabilia for a living, although having seen him knock out a perfect replica of Gary Lineker's signature on a pile of Sports Direct footballs in his living room a couple of years back, I'm not sure how legit most of it is. He is, obviously, a total legend.

Ritz is a fat lad from Birmingham who never stops talking about cars. He drives a motor so suped-up it looks more like a spaceship than a Vauxhall Nova, or whatever it began life as. Every chance he gets he tries to drop something about fucking cars or engines into the conversation. No one's ever been interested, but that never stops him. Like Gaz, he wears clothes that are far too tight for him. Unlike Gaz, it's not because of his muscular frame. It's because he's a fat fucker.

Charlie's been a bit quiet recently. He's going through a bit of dry patch at the moment on the bird front, apart from that dumb bint at the office he's had a couple of times. He's even missed a couple of lads' nights recently. He used to be an absolute hero with the ladies, but something's happened since Christmas. He's gone soft. Started talking about feelings and gay shit like that. He's stopped going out on weeknights as well and started sucking up to David at work. When he was pissed last week he even said he'd like to find someone to settle down with. I don't know what his problem is but he needs to snap out of it quick before I lose my patience.

The mood's a bit flat tonight, so I take it upon myself to get the banter going. I lean in and get the boys to huddle up. "Lads, check out this bird I met up with a couple of weeks ago," I say, as I show them my phone. I scroll through a few pictures from Ava's dating profile. You need to give them something to visualise when you're telling them a story about a girl. She was fit. Obviously. I wouldn't have been meeting her otherwise.

"So we'd been talking online for about a week, right, and then after a few days she sends me a message asking if I want to go round for a movie night," I say, arching my eyebrows for effect, "and we all know what *movie night* means don't we lads?"

"It means a shag," interrupts Gaz, keen to make sure everyone was clear. Like I said, I'm pretty sure he's on some kind of spectrum.

"Cheers, Gaz." I roll my eyes and continue. "So we'd been flirting all week, and the messages had been getting a bit more suggestive. No pictures though which was annoying. I was just about to head over to her gaff, when she sends me another message, telling me to hurry up and get round there. "Obviously," I say, pausing for dramatic effect, "she was gagging for it."

The lads are hanging off every word. Gaz and Ritz high-five each other while Ben shouts 'Wahey' to no one in particular. A few people in the pub give us a few looks. The wankers in here obviously can't handle our banter.

"So I put my foot down and bombed it over there. You can't leave a girl in need can you? She lived in Battersea so only ten minutes away in the Audi. I made a quick stop at Superdrug on the high street though to get some jonnies. A twelve pack. Got to aim for the stars when you're with a new girl haven't you lads?" More laughing, back-slapping and high-fiving. The boys are loving it.

"She came down to meet me when I pulled up. She was wearing these tight little jeans and a vest top. Well casual. Good sign I thought. Easy to take off. She gave me a big smacker on the lips to say hello. She had this deep husky voice. Proper fit she was."

I stop to take a swig of my pint, allowing the tension to rise. Gaz is practically salivating.

"She led me up the stairs to her apartment by the hand. I had a great view of her arse as I walked up behind her. Tight package. We got inside and went straight into the kitchen to grab a drink. I tried it on there and then, but she pushed me away, playing hard to get. I didn't mind though. It just got me going even more."

I pause again. Take a deep breath for effect. The boys are desperate for more details now. I take another gulp of Stella. The gas takes me by surprise and I force out a tiny burp.

"She tells me to go grab a seat in the other room for the movie. Just before I head off to the lounge she says something a bit weird: 'You'd better get in there quick and grab a seat or you'll be standing for the whole film.' I laughed at her. I thought she meant something to do with shagging. So I get into the lounge…"

I pause again. For ages this time. Like I'm Dermot O'Leary reading out the results on X Factor. I look them all in the eye.

"Then what?" cries Ritz. He can't handle the tension. He has to know. The lads are absolutely beside themselves at this point. Confusion and anticipation painted all over their faces. I put them out of their misery.

"Her whole bloody family was sitting there. Her mum, her dad, little brother, even her fucking grandma. She'd actually organized a fucking movie night. With a movie and everything. I couldn't fucking believe it. Ava came in after me and introduced me to everyone. The old dear even shifted up to offer me a space next to her." The boys love it and absolutely piss themselves laughing as I finish off my pint.

"So obviously I needed to get out of there sharpish. I'm not sitting watching a movie with some dickhead's grandma on a first date. Not when I've got a twelve pack burning a hole in my pocket. I told Ava I thought I'd left the car lights on. I shit you not, I must have made it down the stairs and been on the road within about four seconds." The boys piss themselves all over again. "She phoned a couple of time afterwards, but I just blocked her number. I called that barmaid from The Bison and Bird on the way home and went to her place instead."

I bask in the lad's admiration. They can't believe I still managed to get a shag, even after that nightmare. I finish my beer and decide it's time to kick the night into the next gear. The lads whoop and back-slap each other before downing their pints as fast as possible and we make for the exit. Time to find some fanny in Aquum.

We file passed the doormen, and the twenty people waiting in a queue to get in, on account of the fact we know Kev, the manager, from down the gym. Aquum is one of the destination bars of the local area. It's one of those places that likes to think it is dealing with A-list celebrities and footballers in Mayfair. It's even got a little rope at the entrance, as if this somehow makes it more exclusive.

It's empty inside, despite the fact people are being made to wait in a queue outside the front door. House music bounces from the walls. Small pockets of people are already swaying to the beats while they sip their Proseccos and cocktails. The barmen are throwing cocktail shakers around as if they're rock stars playing guitar solos for a baying crowd, not a couple of knob-heads pouring vodka and cokes. They serve twelve-pound cocktails with sparklers in here. They don't serve pints. They serve schooners, which are about a two-thirds of a pint. Obviously they still cost the same as a full pint. When it's full later, it'll be wall to wall with preening, artificially tanned men standing around staring at preening, artificially tanned women. Everyone looking each other over, constantly judging. I absolutely love it.

"Right, who's up for some shots?" shouts Gaz. He shouts everything after a few pints. It can be annoying but there's something endearing about his relentless enthusiasm. The next hour passes in a flash of beers, shots and drinking games. Our voices get thicker and louder. Some birds crowd round nearby, looking to infiltrate our group. We buy them shots and get some banter going, merge their groups into ours. We're well drilled when it comes to this kind of thing. The girls don't stand a chance really. It's normally pretty obvious which chick is interested in which bloke. We don't fight it, we just pair up with the one most likely to result in a shag. Gaz plays the joker card but as always ends up with the worst of the bunch. An absolute whale. Charlie is holding back tonight. Not sure why. One of them's decent and making eyes at him but he's not having any of it.

"You don't recognise me do you?" says one of them to me by the bar. Tall. Dark hair. Big jugs.

I look at her closely, focus as best I can through the cloud of alcohol I'm swimming in. I ogle the frame stood in front of me, hands on hips, and try to work out where I know her from. It hits me. I'm pretty good with faces. And big tits. We went to school together, just around the corner from the where we're standing right now.

"Emma from school!" I blurt at her proudly. She's impressed. I buy her a drink to celebrate our chance reunion. She looks me in the eye as we clink glasses. I know where this is heading. Back to mine.

Turns out I'm wrong. Emma lives a four minute walk away, so we go back there instead.

Chapter Eight

"You're just like your father," says my mum, her voice laced with disappointment. She always manages to phone when I'm fending off a steaming hangover. It's like she's got some kind of sixth sense for it. My mother's greatest fear is that I'll turn out like my dad, moving from girl to girl, wife to wife, and setting up families every few years like some kind of never ending franchise expansion.

I wouldn't know if I was like him of course, as he fucked off on my seventh birthday. While we were singing happy birthday and playing games he was taking half the pictures off the walls. Maybe he thought I'd be too busy blowing out candles to notice. He went to work in a bakery in Dubai a couple of months later, which I never quite got my head around. They've got bakeries over here the last time I looked.

He didn't turn up again until I was fifteen. I used to have to see this therapist, who did my fucking head in. She would always ask me how it made me feel, to not have a Dad around. Over and over again. I said I didn't give a shit. Because I didn't. Not having a dad was normal to me. That was my reality, so why would I give a shit if little Simon down the road had his boring bank manager dad at home for fish fingers and waffles every night? She kept asking though. Again and again. But how does it *make you feel* Danny? Like if she kept asking enough I'd give her the right answer. So she could diagnose me with whatever it said in her textbook.

After four weeks of that I told her she'd get a thump if she asked me again. I didn't have to go back after that. She sent my mum a letter saying I had abandonment issues. What a load of shit. I mean, who doesn't have an issue with being abandoned? Sure, I missed having someone to watch shark documentaries with, but my mum did everything for me. She took me to school, helped me with homework, made my dinner and took me to football at the weekends.

Most of the dads at football were dickheads anyway. I remember one of our games had to be called off because two of them were fighting on the side lines. I was eleven. One of them called the other one's son a 'poof' because he had long hair. Imagine being a grown up and calling an eleven year old a poof. No, I was fine without one of those arseholes thanks very much.

"You haven't had a proper girlfriend since you broke up with Stacey." Five years on and she's still always bringing that up. "You should have kept hold of her, she was a lovely girl."

I never did have the heart to tell my mum that Stacey was the one who left me, not the other way round. In a bizarre mirroring of my dad's behaviour years earlier, she also left me on my birthday. We'd been living together for just over two years and been together for three. I'm not sure why she made the decision to bail out on my birthday. In her defence, she'd long since given up on me turning out how she'd hoped. What had begun as an exciting and passionate relationship slowly degenerated into a miserable bicker-fest. I'm not really sure why we stayed together so long. Months on end filled with snide comments and disapproving glares.

It had taken a while but eventually it dawned on her that the things she assumed I'd grow out of were just my personality traits. She wanted to buy a house and have dinner parties, I wanted to go out with the lads. She wanted to go on holiday to Sardinia but instead I went to Magaluf. I couldn't miss Bazza from work's stag do to be fair. We were just too different and her leaving was for the best. If we'd been honest with each other earlier we could have saved ourselves a lot of time.

I'd also been knocking off this kiwi girl at work for about a year. I think, *I think*, she'd worked that out, which might have had something to do with her attitude towards me. Still, it's a shitty way to spend your birthday, sat on your own in a half-empty house, with boxes of stuff piled around you and hateful words ringing in your ears. The worst part was she took series four of The Wire. I was right in the middle of that.

I've got no intention of getting myself into that kind of situation again. I'm not being pushed into settling down just because it's the normal thing to do. Having to listen to someone tell me I'm not allowed to go out with the lads anymore. Making me go and have lunch with her family every Sunday. Fuck that. I like my life just how it is thanks very much. I've got people I can see when I want a bit of action, but apart from that, I'm free to do whatever the fuck I want. Like shag a girl I haven't seen since school and get a cab home when she passes out.

"What about that Amy girl?" asks my mum, "she seems promising?"

Jesus Christ. It's all I ever hear about. Settling down. I made the mistake of mentioning Amy to get my mum off my back a couple of months ago, but it's had the opposite effect. She keeps banging on about wanting to meet her. The older generation just don't realise it's not like it used to be. You don't leave school, marry someone from down the road when you're twenty-one, gradually grow to hate each other while you chuck out a couple of fucked-up kids anymore. It just doesn't work like that these days.

As is often the case, I feel pretty depressed after a phone-call with my mum. The constant insistence that I'm fucking my life up would chip away at anyone's confidence. Even mine. Sometimes I wonder if I am going to end up like my dad. I do what I always do when I feel like this. I call Amy. Her relentless positivity is always a pick-me-up in times like this.

"Just spoke to my mum," I say. She knows what that means.

She talks me up for the next hour while I lay on my bed. I've fully regressed into a sulking teenager, fresh from a telling off from his mother. She tells me how funny and great to be around I am, which is true, people do love my banter. She tells me how smart I am, which is probably my most underrated attribute, now that she mentions it. Who else would find a way to buy his own flat in Clapham and drive an Audi TT on the pittance Barrie and Aberdeen pay me? She tells me how attractive I am, which it has to be said does seem to be a common viewpoint with women. Most of all she tells me how much she loves spending time with me and wishes we could be together more. She's a good girl Amy, always knows how to raise my spirits. I'm glad she's always there when I need her.

"It sounds like you need a bit of a break," she says. Maybe a bit of sun would do you good?" The thought hadn't really occurred to me. The last time I went away was a weekend in Krakow with the lads, over a year ago now. One-pound-twenty a pint and a fiver a lap dance. Fucking great banter that was.

"Yeah," I say, "maybe you're right." I wonder if the lads would be up for another trip. Kavos, or Marbella, maybe Ayia Napa. Or even better a week in Ibiza trawling San Antonio for young birds and pilling our tits off. That would be a right laugh. Like the good old days.

"Maybe we could do a trip together," she asks. Christ I didn't see that one coming. "A week in Spain, something cheap and cheerful. Just the two of us."

"Maybe," I say, as non-committal as possible. The thought doesn't completely repulse me. I'll need to check with the lads first, see if they're up for a week away somewhere. But a week with Amy somewhere would be alright. She's got good banter, for a bird, and I'd be guaranteed a shag every night. It'd be a decent backup.

"Yeah," I say to her, "I'll think about it."

"Amazing," she says.

Typical Amy. Always positive.

Chapter Nine

"Can you help Mrs Baker please Danny?" David's monotone interrupts me midway through a particularly intense sexting session with Michelle. Maybe it's my sky-high blood pressure from the graphic description of what she's got planned for the next time we see each other, but Mrs Baker immediately grabs my attention. She's fit. A proper milf. Well-groomed dark hair down to her shoulders, toned body, expensive clothes. She's probably one of those yummy-mummy types that drop the kids off at school every morning then fills her empty days up with exercise classes at the gym to keep herself in shape. I bet she's banged a personal trainer or two in her time.

"Please, take a seat," I stammer, dropping my phone on the desk like a hot kebab. Bad timing, as Michelle's just sent me a video clip. That will have to wait until lunchtime. I shift the weight on my chair in an attempt to ensure my protruding hard-on is obscured from view by the desk. I'm not sure if it works. Mrs Baker's plunging neckline doesn't do much to reduce the problem. She flicks her hair back from her shoulders. She looks amused. I think the tent in my pants has been rumbled. "So, how can I help you?" I ask, still mindful of the bulge beneath my desk.

"I'd like to put my house on the market as soon as possible." She doesn't mess about. Urgent and business-like. I like it. I imagine she'd call the shots in the bedroom. Bet she knows exactly what she likes. The experienced type. She goes on to explain that she recently caught her, quote, *prick of a husband*, in bed with their twenty-one year old Polish au pair. "I came home early from work and found them in the shower together," she says. "The bitch didn't even apologise. She just looked at me and smiled while she towelled herself off."

I try not to picture it while she's still talking.

"I want to draw a line under this and move on as soon as possible," she says.

"Ah," I say, "I'm sorry to hear about all that." I'm not sure how best to respond. I want to offer a cheeky comment painting Mr Baker as a fool. I reckon she'd like that. Mrs Baker is clearly top-notch. For her age anyway. But to be fair, I haven't seen the au pair so I can't in all fairness make a judgement on the geezer's decision making. I take some details down instead. Keep it professional. Ignore how easy it would be to feed her a line.

Her house is on a decent road on the outskirts of Clapham. They've owned it for six years so it's probably doubled in value since they've been living there. They'll be no shortage of potential viewings once I get it on the market. She'll get her wish to move on pretty quickly and a tidy sum to do it with.

"Does your husband know you're selling the place?" I ask.

"He's not going to argue if he wants to see his kids again," she says, a darkness clouding her eyes. The anger is still bubbling, barely beneath the surface. She'd definitely be great in the sack.

I move the conversation on before the brain in my pants starts leading me in a different direction. "I can come and do a valuation for you sometime this week if that works? It won't take long. We can have it on the market within a couple of days and be doing viewings right away?"

"Better make it Friday." she replies. "The kids will be out all day so we won't be disturbed." She stares me straight in the eyes and says; "You can take all the time you need." She's got a naturally flirty tone to her, so I'm not sure if her comment is loaded with intent or if it's just the last remnants of my pulsing erection affecting my brain. She stands and offers her hand, which lingers a second or two longer than necessary. I get the slightest wink from her as she looks back at me on her way out the door. There's definitely something there. Mrs Baker would be the ultimate rebound shag. She'd make the likes of Sophie last week look like an amateur. I'd probably need an ambulance afterwards.

David marches straight over to my desk as soon as she's left, intent on completely ruining my buzz. "Charlie mentioned something about a house over near Green Lane? I haven't seen any details yet Danny, where are they?"

Shit. He means Mrs O'Shea's place. I glance over at Charlie who shrugs apologetically. He's dropped me right in it and he knows it. "Don't worry yourself Dave, I've already got a buyer lined up."

He flinches at Dave. I know he hates it but sometimes I can't help myself. "You have a buyer lined up, but it's yet to go on the market?" he speaks at me slowly, like I'm a Spanish shopkeeper on his yearly holiday to Torremolinos.

I speak slowly back. "I called one of my investors Dave. He came to see it straight away. Just waiting for the survey now."

"You know the process Danny," he signs. He's disappointed. "It's there for a reason. We don't want another Dixon Street on our hands do we?"

Fucking Dixon Street. Jesus Christ is he going to bang on about that for the rest of his miserable life?

Sure, there was a bit of aggro last year when we sold the house for the old man and his kids turned up and started complaining. And yes, the sale price was well below market value. But that's the cost of a quick sale. The greedy shit of a son and his gold-digger wife were only up in arms about it because they were already counting their inheritance. Ok, so the ombudsman was called in, and there was that little bit of press coverage, but he didn't find anything conclusively dodgy, so what was the problem? We were cleared of any wrongdoing. The old man got some money for his shit-tip of a house, Nick got a cheap property and we got the commission. Sure, I got a brown envelope filled with twenties but that's the game we're in. His bloodsucking kids would just have to get in line to take their piece of the pie.

I can't be arsed with the hassle today though so I decide to let him have this one. I don't want David sticking his nose in any more than he already is. "No, David, you're right, we don't want another Dixon Street. I'll get all the details online this afternoon."

He smiles. He's pleased I'm toeing the line. I head straight outside and get on the phone to Jimmy. He's going to need to get a shift on with that survey. If that place goes on the open market we'll be right in the shit.

David walks about with a smug grin on his face for the next couple of hours, like he's the king of the fucking castle, so I make up that I've got some viewings booked in and make my way down to Headmasters for a hair chop. It's been three weeks so I'm overdue. I normally prefer to get it done every couple of weeks, to make sure I'm always on top of my game. Also, one of the hairdressers in there is a tidy sort. All tan and blonde extensions. She's showing a bit of side-boob today as well, which I'm personally a big fan of. She'll likely get a fiver tip today just for that.

I sit in the little reception area while I wait for her to stop making small talk with some old codger. The thing I like about this place is they have loads of decent old magazines. Loaded, FHM and Maxim. You can't get them anymore which is a bit gutting. I used to love heading down the corner shop and picking up a stash every Saturday. Proper good they were. Jugs, gadgets, jokes, they had everything really. Shame they stopped making them but I guess people go online if they want to see a picture of Gillian Anderson's tits these days.

Chapter Ten

Some tenants turn up in the office on Tuesday morning with a carrier bag full of letters for the old owner. Quite what they want me to do with them I don't know. What am I, the fucking postman? We sold the place to their landlord about three months ago. The previous owner was some fifty-year old who'd spunked all his redundancy money thinking he was going to make it rich in property. I can probably dig out a forwarding address from somewhere if I really have to. I thank the idiot tenants for being so considerate as I walk them to the front door.

I tear open the first envelope as soon as I'm back at my desk. Reading through people's old mail is one of my favourite things to do. It's a real window into their private lives. You see some classic stuff. And the occasional awful thing as well to be fair. It's brilliant. Better than any episode of EastEnders.

"You shouldn't be doing that," whines Alice, "It's illegal."

I roll my eyes and tell her to go fuck herself. She looks like she's going to bawl it. Honestly, sometimes I think the only reason she's here is because of that rack of hers. I grin at Charlie. He doesn't say anything. Just looks at me. I keep forgetting he doinked her a few weeks back.

It turns out the old owner had some serious debt problems. Letters from credit card companies, overdue gas bills, even a threatening letter from QuickQuid. When those fucker's are threatening you with the bailiffs you know you're in the shit. No wonder he was in such a rush to sell. The bloke dropped off the face of the earth as soon as the money hit his account. There's also a big brown envelope marked 'private and confidential'. Those are always the best ones. I'm so keen to get into it I rip some of the paper inside. Some test results from his doctor. He's got something nasty by the sounds of it. Should probably get that seen to sharpish.

There was a time back in the day, when I was a bit more unscrupulous, that I might have passed all these details onto an old schoolmate of mine with a penchant for identity theft, but I'm done with all that now. The police started sniffing around a couple of years back. Not really worth the risk for a few quid here and there. I just read through this stuff for the laughs now. Besides, there's no point in stealing the identity of someone whose credit's already fucked. Kind of defeats the point. I dump the letters in the drawer of my desk along with any other redirected mail that's found its way to me and get to work on putting Mrs O'Shea's house online.

I'm still stalling for Nick, so I only put it on Zoopla. If it's not on Rightmove you may as well not bother. I still get a couple of calls though. Those knob-heads Marcus and Jo-Jo are the first. She wants to organise a viewing this afternoon. I can't be bothered to listen to her reciting phrases she's heard off Homes Under The Hammer, and I need to buy my surveyor mate a bit of time, so I put them in the diary for Friday, and make up some bullshit excuse about needing the place to be vacant before we can do any viewings. Nick calls. He's seen it online and wants to know what the fuck is going on. I reassure him, tell him it's not on Rightmove yet, and I'll make sure it won't be for a while. He's not happy though. I let him bang on at me for a bit. Anyone else and I'd tell them to fuck off in no uncertain terms, but I need to keep Nick sweet if I'm going to keep myself in the style I've become accustomed to.

Another investment opportunity presents itself only two hours later. A young bloke stumbles into the office, hair all over the place, bags under his eyes. Some posh twat named Jonty. He's looking to offload a flat he rents out to students nearby. He's wearing the standard jumped-up property investor garb; jeans, t-shirt, shoes, blazer, looking like he owns Facebook or Google or something. He's probably paid a couple of grand for one of those property investor seminars, bought a flat and thought he'd got it made. Big mistake. The bloke looks like he hasn't slept in weeks. If you looked up stressed in the dictionary, there'd be a picture of this dickhead staring back at you.

Students are a nightmare, I've no idea why anyone bothers renting to them. They always trash the place. I bet he's sick of having to deal with them. Students are all a bunch of hippy tax-dodgers these days as well. Always offended about something. Always protesting or marching, normally about gays or tampons or some shit. Not like in my day. We just got pissed, played Mario Kart and got on with it. Like you're supposed to. He's only had the place a year, bought it for four-twenty. I tell him I'll come and take a look at it this week and I'll do everything I can to help him out. Depending on how much of a moron this bloke is, it could be a nice potential backup for Nick if the O'Shea deal goes tits up. I'd go and check it out this afternoon, but I need to shoot off early to get the Audi washed.

Now you can say what you want about the Poles, but they don't half give a car a good scrubbing. About twelve of the fuckers descend upon it as soon as I roll up and it looks brand spanking new ten minutes later. Six quid. Unbelievable. I normally do it on Sundays but I pushed it back a couple of days this week. I've got a date with a posh bird tonight and nothing impresses them more than a gleaming sports car. That and a fat wedge of cash.

I've been talking to Verity for a few weeks now. Truth be told, I'm not that keen, but I've got no one better to date tonight, so I thought fuck it. She's a bit pushy for my liking as well. Very insistent that we go out for dinner. I normally like to avoid that on a first date, unless the chick's an absolute stonewall ten out of ten. Verity's not quite at that level. She's a seven from what I can tell from her pictures. She's picked somewhere swanky down by the river in Battersea. No doubt I'll be the one picking up the tab. The location's a bit annoying as it's a bit too far to get her back to mine quickly if things are going well. Who knows though, if all goes to plan maybe I'll get noshed off in the front seat. It wouldn't be the first time and you can always bank on a posh bird to be dirty.

Chapter Eleven

I pick up Verity outside her flat, some gated community down by the river, not far from the restaurant. Despite the February temperature, she's wearing a very short dress, which I appreciate. She's making up for her lack of coverage downstairs with a fur coat and some kind of silky scarf up top. She absolutely reeks of Daddy's money.

I get out and open the door for her. I get an air-kiss by way of a hello. The sort that people only do if they're loaded. Or French. I play along, even though I feel like a right cock. She directs me the three hundred metres or so to the restaurant in the way someone does who's used to having a chauffeur ferry her about. She's pissing me off but she's quite fit so I let it slide. I've met birds like this before. They're all the same. I know how to get what I want from them.

We're greeted by an exceptionally tidy hostess who takes us to our table. I paid a bit extra and reserved one overlooking the waterfront. Verity's impressed. Like I say, they're all the same these types. A waiter brings us over a glass of champagne with the menus. She's already purring.

I feel my phone vibrating in the pocket of my Thomas Pink blazer, which I bought for the occasion, so I excuse myself and head to the men's room. I answer the phone while I'm at the urinal. Might as well kill two birds with one stone while I'm in here. It's Amy.

"I've been trying to get hold of you all evening," she says, "where are you?"

This is the issue with Amy. She seems to think we're in a relationship. Sure, we see each other every week and speak to each other most days on the phone, but I've been very clear from day one that I'm not looking to get into anything serious. I just don't think things need to be labelled in this day and age. We aren't in the fifties for Christ's sake. We argued about it a lot a few months ago but she doesn't bring it up anymore. We just have our regular Friday nights together and leave it at that. This doesn't stop her from panicking when she can't get hold of me. She's got this fear of me going out with other girls, which is another thing I like to avoid talking about.

"I'm at the pub with the lads." I lie. "I left my phone in the car, sorry."

"Why have you got your car at the pub?" she asks, like she's fucking Columbo or something.

"Ritz is checking the exhaust," I say, "it's been playing up all week. Keeps making a rattling sound." I'm a hell of a liar, it's one of my true gifts in life. The words just roll off the tongue.

"Oh ok," she says, taking my word for it. "I just wanted to remind you about Holly's birthday on Friday. You said you'd come. Please don't let me down."

"Of course I won't," I say, "I'll be there." I need to get her off the phone sharpish or Verity will think I'm in here taking a massive dump.

"I'd better go," I say, "the lads are waiting."

"Ok babe," she says, despite the fact I hate her calling me that, "say hi to the lads for me."

I hang up the phone after giving my hands a cursory rinse, I haven't got time for the full soap and water job, and rush back to the table. "Sorry about that," I say to Verity, who looks like she's chewing on a wasp. "Had the office on the phone, they needed my approval on a big deal."

She perks up at the sound of this. "What is it you do again Daniel?" No one's called me Daniel since I was about nine.

"I own a chain of estate agent's," I lie. "Barrie and Aberdeen, you may have seen us around the Clapham area."

She's interested again. Thinks I'm minted. These posh birds are so predictable.

We spend the rest of the evening talking about her. She rides horses, out in the sticks somewhere in Surrey, which is a difficult one for me. On the one hand, horsey people tend to have incredibly firm thighs and arse-cheeks, and those riding trousers they wear really get me going. On the other hand, they tend to be total arseholes. I'm not going to be hanging around after this evening though so I don't suppose that matters. She's a solicitor for some famous firm up in town. They defend loads of high-profile celebs when they've fucked up. The job sounds dull but I bet she hears some cracking rumours. I try to get some out of her but she's having none of it.

We order sorbet for dessert, which I've never had before. It's basically shit ice-cream. Verity doesn't move a muscle when the bill arrives. She doesn't even do that *pretend-to-want-to-go-halves* thing. Evidently Verity gets taken care of by the men in her life. If she's lucky she'll get properly taken care of tonight. I pay by peeling off six twenties from the stack I've wedged into my jacket pocket. I've even bought a silver money clip especially for tonight. "I like to deal in cash," I say to her as she tries unsuccessfully not to gawp at the remaining bundle. That seems to swing it and she's sticking her tongue down my throat as soon as we get down to the car.

"Do you want to come up?" she breathes into my ear as we pull up outside her flat.

Her apartment is top drawer. She opens a bottle of Prosecco and hands me a glass. I've got my eyes on those thighs of hers as we sit down on the leather sofa. It's only five minutes before I've got my hands on them in the bedroom. Or the master bedroom, as she likes to call it. As if we're in Daddy's mansion back home, not a two bed flat. Albeit a very nice one.

Her thighs and arse-cheeks are as firm as I'd hoped. The upside of all that horse-riding bollocks. I get the impression this is the first time in a while for her, as she's frantic in her attempts to get my boxers off. Unfortunately we barely get to second base as she's pretty frantic when it comes to everything else as well and I begin to wonder if she's going to do permanent damage. Maybe she should have spent more time learning how to fumble with a bloke's gear instead of all that time riding around on horses. I have to take evasive action after about a minute before she amputates my knob. I stop her. Tell her this is all moving too fast. That I think we should wait. That I don't want to ruin things by diving into anything. She's gagging for it so she's not happy. Throws her toys right out the pram. She tries to seduce me into changing my mind but there's no way that's happening. I'll end up in A&E.

I make it home in ten minutes flat and head straight for the frozen peas. It's nearly midnight. Chris comes out to ask how the date went. He sees me icing my cock on the sofa, raises an eyebrow. "Date went that well did it?" he says.

Chapter Twelve

I manage to get down to Stresshead's flat on Thursday morning. It's a good size but it's a right state and no mistake. There's only three students in there but it's like a family of twenty's been squatting for the whole year. Absolute carnage.

The hallway is full of festering sports kit, stinking the place right out. I pick my way over the bags and boots and get to the living room. There's a wall of beer cans on one side. Fosters, all of them. They cover the smallest wall of the rectangular room, and spill over into a line along the skirting boards of the longest wall. Impressive. Stresshead shows me around the rest of the warzone, moaning about the tenants as we tiptoe our way through the debris, moving in and out of each of the bedrooms. He's managed to get himself a decent flat here, he'd be mental to sell it now, the market's booming. It'll be worth another hundred grand in a year or so. Not that I tell him that. This is just a recon mission to find out how dumb he is.

We take a seat on one of the sofas in the living room. He wants to know if he'll get all the money back he's sunk into the place. I'm not sure if he knows it, but the market has shot up over the last year. This place is probably worth about five hundred now.

If I can convince him that the students have done a fair bit of damage, but that I might be able to get him somewhere near to what he paid for it, it should just about work for Nick. People are always scared of a bit of damage. Sure, there's beer cans everywhere and a couple of minor holes in the wall. There's a bit of mould in the bathroom and while we're sitting in the living room I notice a slice of pizza stuck to the lampshade, but it'll cost a couple of grand tops to get it good as new. If I could get this for Nick for four-hundred, he'd be laughing, and I'd be picking up another envelope full of cash. I tell Stresshead I'll get back to him early next week with a valuation, which gives me time to sound Nick out.

I chase Jimmy about the survey for Mrs O'Shea's gaff on Friday morning. The dickhead's gone on holiday until Wednesday next week without putting the wheels in motion. Nick's raging and gives me a right bollocking down the phone. It's been over a week and nothing's happened yet. David's crawling all over me as well, as I've still not got it live on Rightmove. I've given him the classic *technical issues* excuse but I think he knows I'm stalling. Especially as he's caught me on my computer at least three times this week looking at potential destinations for a lads' holiday. Got to get some research done before I speak to the boys about it tomorrow.

I give David's eagle eyes the slip as I need to get over to Mrs Baker's place to do the valuation. If I can get her place sold quickly then I'll make a bit of ground up on Charlie. He sold another flat this morning, the lucky prick. He's on a real roll at the moment. If I'm not on my game that five grand is going to slip through my fingers.

Mrs Baker's place is like a ghost house when I get there. There's cardboard boxes everywhere. The walls are bare, with dusty outlines of pictures all over the place. Everything's been taken down in a hurry. What was obviously a family home looks like an empty shell now. I guess if you find out your husband's been banging the au pair you don't want to see family pictures grinning down at you when you're sitting on the toilet.

The recycling bin is full of empty wine bottles. Mrs Baker obviously isn't taking the whole thing very well. She offers me a glass. I decline, it's only ten-thirty. And anyway, I'm driving. I can't afford to get done for that again.

She gives me the guided tour. Living room. Dining room. Kitchen and conservatory. The utility room hums with the sound of the spinning washing machine. Two bathrooms upstairs, one's an en suite, the other a family bathroom, populated with children's toothbrushes and bathing products. Some Matey bubble bath sits on the side and a toy boat lies marooned on the bottom of the empty bathtub. Three bedrooms. One's the kids' room judging from the bunk beds. They've got Star Wars bedclothes that remind me of when I shared a room with my little brother. The master bedroom is untidy. Ruffled bed sheets. Pile of men's shirts in the corner. Some of them have had the sleeves cut off. There's another bottle of wine, half-drunk, by the bed. The whole place looks like a bomb's hit it, which I guess it kind of has. The other bedroom is smaller. It's completely empty. Like no one has ever been in there. I suspect this may have been where the au pair used to stay. I look back at the bunk beds and wonder how the kids are feeling. They won't know what's happened or understand it at all. They'll just know their dad's not around anymore.

Mrs Baker's wearing a shirt that's barely buttoned up. No bra underneath, leaving very little to the imagination. I can see she's in good nick. Obviously spends a lot of time down the gym. I suspect she's had a bit of surgery here and there as well, because her tits are doing their best to burst out of the shirt with the kind of fury that only money can buy. She lingers in the doorway of her bedroom as I take in the dimensions. She comes up close and asks me if I like what I see? She's biting her lip and it's on a plate and I can tell by the look in her eye that it'd be a chance worth taking, but a cloud of heartbreak hangs over the house and I can't get the kids' bedroom out of my head. I step back slightly, decline under the pretence of professionalism.

"Maybe another time," I say, "when the house has been sold." It's a terrible, gut-wrenching situation, but you've got to leave the door open when a pair like that are on offer. I shuffle back to the car attempting to hide the raging boner in my trousers from any passers-by.

"How was it?" asks David when I'm back.

"Nice layout," I say, "shouldn't be hard to find someone interested." I sit at my desk and try unsuccessfully to put Mrs Baker out of my mind. I already regret not taking advantage of her offer. Charlie and Alice have been doing the paperwork for one of his sales all afternoon. She's fussing around him like a new puppy. It's doing my head in. I head out the door on the dot of five so I've got time for a shower before I meet up with Amy for her sister's birthday.

*****

"So this is the secret boyfriend we've heard so much about?"

I flinch. Amy goes bright red.

"Can I have a word with you?" I say to her, quietly. We head outside for a moment, away from the festivities, and her mum who's the one who's just used the B word.

"What the fuck Amy?" I say. I don't really need to elaborate any further as she's already scrabbling around, frantically trying to calm me down. I've met her sister, Holly, a couple of times before. They were out together when Amy and I first met. Before we'd even organised our first date. She's a decent sort. Not as fit as Amy but a nice girl. Good banter. It's a Friday night, which I always spend with Amy, so I could hardly say I was doing something else. It's Holly's thirtieth, one of those birthdays girls always make a big deal about. So I didn't mind meeting up with her and her dozy boyfriend Adrian. I thought if I put in an appearance tonight I'd get some serious brownie points with Amy, which she normally pays in sexual favours.

I did not expect to turn up to the pub to find half of Amy's fucking family waiting for me. It's a full on ambush. She knew I'd never come if she'd told me this mob were all going to be here.

Despite the shock, I managed to be polite when I arrived and gave Holly a big happy birthday hug and shook hands with Adrian, even though I could see them all around the room, eyeing me up the second I got in there. Her mum steamed over before Amy had the chance to explain herself.

"*The secret boyfriend*," I say to her, "for fuck's sake."

"I'm sorry," she blurts, "I didn't think you'd come if I told you they'd all be here, and I really wanted you to be here with me."

I just stare at her.

"I'm sorry," she says again. We look at each other for a few seconds. I can see she's worried I'm going to leg it. She needn't worry, I wouldn't be that much of an arsehole. Not to her anyway. "I'll make it up to you," she says.

I'm just about to start negotiating *exactly* how she's going to make it up to me, when an old woman approaches us.

"Hello dear," says the old biddy.

"Hi Grandma," she says, "so glad you could make it."

"And who's this young man?" says Grandma.

This is going to be a long evening.

It turns out her dad's the only real pain in the arse of the lot. He grills me for a while about my intentions towards Amy. Smart geezer. He eases off after a few beers. He's a good bloke. Supports Arsenal but I let him off. Been building for forty years and had his own firm the last twenty-five. Good, honest, salt of the earth type. Rips me for being an estate agent. Says he doesn't trust them. Obviously knows the score. Amy's mum is a great old girl. Done up to the nines for Holly's big night. She's from another era, spent most of her life looking after her husband. She can't half put away the gin though. We all sit down and tuck into some pub food. The drinks keep flowing and I'm surprised to find I'm enjoying myself. I can tell by the grin plastered across Amy's face that she's noticed it as well.

"You still owe me," I whisper to her with a wink. She squeezes my hand. She's happy. I guess I am too.

Chapter Thirteen

I'm down the pub with the lads just before Soccer Saturday starts. I put a round of Stellas on the table and I tell them there's something I want to discuss with them. They know this because I told them to get here early because of something big. They look nervous. Like I'm going to announce I've got Aids or something. Ritz unwraps one of the emergency pork pies he keeps in his jacket pocket and slowly pops it into his mouth, not taking his eyes off me for a second. He always stuffs his face when he's stressed. Well, he stuffs his face for any reason really, which is why he's a fat fucker.

The lads lean in towards me. "One word," I say, "Marbs." I let it sink in. I don't say anything else. I don't need to. Grins spread across their faces like a Mexican wave at an England friendly.

"All of us this summer. One week in Marbella, chasing birds, getting smashed and absolutely having it at Lineker's and Nikki Beach," I say as they gawp at me like I've just told them they've won the lottery. I raise my glass in a toast. "Lads on tour."

"Lads on tour," they chorus in unison. Ritz chokes on his pork-pie, before forcing it down and joining in the toast with a belated shout of *lads on tour*. Gaz looks like he is going to explode. He's always wanted to go to Marbella. I swear he thinks the streets are paved with gold. He stands up and simply shouts, "Marbs" with a big shit-eating smile across his face and his arms outstretched.

"We are going to get so fucked," chimes in Ben. For a sexual deviant like Ben, Marbella's paradise. Herd after herd of naïve, middle-class eighteen year olds on their first girls' holiday and thick as shit Essex girls with it all hanging out. All of them completely trusting the gangs of blokes queuing up to pour vodka shots down their necks and invite them back to after-parties at their apartments. Blokes like Ben and me.

"Can we stay in the centre?" asks Gaz, "Right next to Lineker's?"

"Whatever you want, Gaz." I say. "Whatever you want."

"Fucking hell," he says wistfully. I'd love to see the picture forming inside that empty head of his. "I'm getting some shots in," he says, leaping to his feet.

"Not for me thanks, mate." says Charlie, pissing right on Gaz's parade. "It's only lunchtime."

"Come on geez," begs Gaz. "We're going to Marbs! It's going to be awesome. We need to celebrate."

"Just the one then," he replies.

"What's the matter, mate?" I say, eyeing Charlie. "Not up for it? Can't handle the banter? Not got the minerals for a lads' holiday in Marbella?"

I've had my eye on him since I said the magic word. He's not as excited as the rest. There's something holding him back.

"Not at all mate," he says, all defensive. He clinks my pint with his. "Lads on tour," he says. He smiles, but with his mouth not his eyes. Like someone important just made a shit joke and you have to pretend to find it funny.

Gaz returns with a tray of Sambucas. We knock them back and Ben starts a chant of *Lads on Tour, Lads on Tour, Lads on Tour* to the tune of the old football classic *here we go*. It grows in volume until we start getting evils from a couple of old bastards at the bar. I tell them to fuck off. Charlie gets another round in before ducking out to go to some family thing. He's high-fiving everyone on his way out the door. He's a decent actor. He's got all the boys fooled. All of them except me.

The rest of us get proper smashed. Stellas and Sambucas with every round until last orders. We end up getting chucked out of the pub when I tell the miserable old fuckers I'll clump them if they keep eyeballing us. Bunch of wankers.

We head down to Inferno's and do well to get in. Ritz is slurring and Gaz drops about seven hundred coins on the floor as we're paying the entrance fee. Ben knows the drill and just keeps quiet, doesn't look any of the doormen in the eye. I can barely see straight but we've been here so many times it's instinctive. Through the corridor, tenner to the girl on reception, up the stairs and straight into the action. We trawl around the place, picking up another round of beers on the way, before huddling around one of the dancefloors.

There's a couple of pissed up birds on the two podiums. One of them's a right munter, I can tell that even in my battered state. The other one's passable. Tiny skirt. You can see her knickers from where we're standing. Which is probably why there's a huddle of about thirty blokes watching her. She knows it as well the dirty minx and spends a good hour flashing everyone her G-string. Every other girl in the place is disgusted. I hear at least four calling her a slag.

I bump into Emma from school again. She's a bit pissed off that I didn't say goodbye to her when I left her flat last weekend, but she was out for the count and I didn't want to wake her. She's also not impressed that I didn't call her this week, but I buy her another shot to make up for it.

She forgives me pretty quick, mainly because she's blatantly after another seeing to. She's all over me but by this point I'd be no use to her anyway, so I take a rain check and promise to call her. Maybe I will, if I get proper fucking desperate. Unlikely though. She was average in the sack. Held too much back. Didn't give it her best shot.

The way I look at it, if you're on trial at Man United, you don't play it safe, keep it nice and simple. You get your best tricks out, show all your skills off. She didn't do that, so she didn't pass the trial. That's just the way it goes.

By twelve-thirty Gaz has dropped at least three beers down himself and Ritz is drowning in sweat. Ben's gone off with some milf he attached himself to pretty sharpish after we arrived. She was horrible but he's the only one who's pulled so I guess the jokes on us. We can barely stand up so we call it quits and stumble across to the kebab shop for a doner before we all go our separate ways. The geezer behind the counter plays a bit fast and loose with the chilli sauce which I suspect will come back to haunt me in the morning. Gaz hugs us all as we say our goodbyes, then heads off down the high street singing at the top of his voice. Safe to say he's excited about the lads' trip.

Chapter Fourteen

"Alright lad," I say to Charlie as he walks into the office on Monday morning, "I'm proper buzzing for Marbs. Going to have a look online this morning for some deals."

Alice looks over. "Off to Marbella are you?" she pipes up from somewhere behind that massive rack of hers. It's only us three in the office today. David's at some management offsite somewhere. God knows what Colin's up to.

"Yep," I say, "Lads on tour in Marbs. Should be proper fucking mental."

She doesn't say anything else for the rest of the morning, thank fuck. I spend most of it on the teletext website looking at apartments. I reckon we can get something for about three-hundred each for the week. The places look pretty rank but they're slap bang in the middle of the action, five minutes from Lineker's. Absolutely perfect. It's not like we're going to be inside much anyway. The lads will just have to make sure they bang a few posh birds if they want a decent shower in the morning. It's still a couple of weeks until pay day, but until then I'm making a list of the potential options, so we can get it all booked up sharpish. I head over to Charlie's desk about eleven and get him to bring up the top three I've sent him so far.

"What do you reckon?" I say, "They're pretty basic but they'll do."

Alice comes over while we're sitting there looking at his computer screen. "When are you thinking of going?" she asks.

"In a couple of months' time." I say, "When the opening parties are starting up at Ocean Club and Nikki Beach." Charlie's staring silently at the screen. He's probably cracking a boner at the thought of all the slags we're going to be tucking into.

"Whatever," she says, "I'm off to do a viewing." She heads back to her desk and picks up her bag. I notice her arse is looking pretty good today as she walks out the door.

"I might dash out for an early lunch actually," says Charlie. He must be starving as he absolutely legs it out a few seconds later. It's not even eleven-thirty yet. He can be fucking weird sometimes Charlie. It's just me in the office now, so I use the opportunity to give Jonty Stresshead a call about his flat. I tell him I've done some research and taking into account the damage, which is quite substantial, I reckon if we put his flat on at four-hundred we can get a quick sale. He doesn't exactly bite my hand off, but says he'll have a think about it before he comes in to discuss it with me. I drop Nick another text to let him know I might have another fish hooked on the line.

"Another one already?" he sends back. At this rate I might need to speak to him about a bigger cut. The geezer's making millions off me.

*****

Despite the fact I royally went to town on her only a week ago, Michelle is very insistent that we go out on a proper date. It's annoying and a total waste of time but she was top-drawer in the sack so I agree. Besides, a decent shag on an otherwise dull Tuesday night is not to be sniffed at.

I'm sure it won't take long to pick up where we left off last time, so I arrange to meet her at The Duck. Hopefully it'll only take one drink, maximum two before she's ready to get cracking again. What girls like Michelle fail to understand is that if they put out on the first date, there's nothing for me to chase. Nothing for me to make an effort for. If she thinks I'm going to take the time to get to know her after we've already boned she's very much mistaken. That first night defined our relationship. It's about one thing: sex. There's no coming back from that.

She's late, which is a bad start. We said seven and it's already ten past. No *'sorry I'm running late'* text or anything like that. Infuriating. She rushes in just before quarter past. Any longer than that and I'd have canned the whole thing. But she's here now so I let it slide. No apology, but she is looking exceptionally fit so I immediately forgive her poor time-keeping.

She's wearing a similar dress to her speed-dating ensemble, this time in blue. There's so much cleavage on show she'd probably be arrested in some countries. Michelle clearly knows where her strengths lie. I respect that. She rabbits on about work, all the difficult clients she's had at the salon this week, what a bitch one of the other girls is, how the pay's shit, that sort of thing. I sip my pint and stare at her tits. She takes a breath, finally, and gulps down some Pinot.

"So," I say, grateful for the opportunity to speak, "speed dating was fun."

She's not embarrassed or fazed in the slightest. "Sure was," she says, "I've got my toothbrush and some knickers with me for the morning. I figured we'd want to have some fun again tonight."

I'm beginning to like Michelle.

We head for the door as soon as we've finished our drinks. The barman in here already thinks I'm some sort of magician but tonight's a new record even by my standards. Michelle only got here twelve minutes ago.

It doesn't take long to get her clothes off, as she's not wearing any underwear. Another gold star for Michelle. If anything, she's even more appallingly behaved tonight. She's got real talent. I mean, it's never going to be a long-term thing, she's thick as shit with terrible banter for a start, but she's a tremendous addition to my list of options.

We finally give it a rest just before one-thirty. A full five hours after I first whipped her dress off. Poor old Chris must be sick of the sound of her already. I feel like I've been a few rounds with Mike Tyson. I check my phone when she's asleep and see a couple of missed calls from Amy. Better not to get back to her now. It'd only arouse suspicion. I'll give her a call in the morning and tell her my phone was playing up. Make out that I didn't get her missed calls.

My last thought before I drift off is that there is no way Michelle can keep up this level of performance. The intensity's sure to drop off at some point. I'll need to make sure we only see each other every few weeks to make the most of it before I get bored.

Chapter Fifteen

Despite the urgency, its Thursday morning before Jimmy gets back in touch with the survey for O'Shea's place. He finally managed to get over to the house yesterday. Now he just needs to type it up and get it sent over. He didn't actually need to go over there obviously, he's putting whatever I want him to on the valuation, but it all helps to add to the professional charade. It needs to look above board in case anyone starts sniffing around asking questions.

Nick's been all over me now it's on the open market, thanks to David and his fucking rules. I managed to hold off putting it on Rightmove until yesterday morning, but as soon as it went live the calls piled in. I've got a couple of viewings today and David's crawling up my arse every few minutes for an update. If I can avoid one of these two putting an offer in and Jimmy gets the survey over to me by the end of play, I can legitimately take it back off the market. Sale agreed. Job done. It's bloody stressful but it'll be worth it when that fat envelope full of twenties is in my pocket.

I meet the first viewing at the property just after lunch. A young couple. She's fit. He's batting well above his average. They must be doing alright if they can afford a place like this. The bloke's younger than me as well. A bit jumped up for my liking. His wife's cooing all over the shop the second we get through the door. Banging on about how it's got that family home feel about it. Already earmarking one of the rooms for a nursery no doubt. I get the impression she's probably already hiding the contraceptive pills. No prizes for guessing who wears the trousers in their relationship. Poor bastard.

I need to think on my feet and throw her off the scent before she's got him writing a cheque out here and now. An offer from these yuppie pricks would be a right spanner in the works. I tell them how sad it is that the property is even on the market. That the owner died in his sleep in this very room only last week. That chills her boots immediately. She can't get out of the bedroom quick enough. There's nothing quite like the shadow of death hanging over a place to put off a younger buyer. It's like they think the old boy's going to haunt them just for moving into his house. They cut the viewing short after no more than a cursory look around the rest, not even bothering to check out the massive garden. That's the problem with these young types with more money than sense. Everything put them off. Not like someone like Nick. There could be a children's dungeon in the basement and he'd see it as an opportunity to snap up a bargain.

The dead old man story worked so well I roll it straight out to the next viewing, but he's a hardier soul. A fat bloke in jeans and a t-shirt. Builder of some sort. Doesn't bat an eyelid. Starts asking about the age of the boiler, fence boundaries and the likelihood of getting planning permission for an extension. Christ. I've got a live one on my hands here. No imaginary stench of death is going to put this bloke off.

Luckily I've got a little something in my repertoire for every eventuality. I chuck in the word subsidence and he recoils like I've just shat on the carpet. Can't get out of the place quick enough, as if the very mention of the word is enough to make the walls start crumbling around us, like he's Leonardo Di Caprio in that film Inception. I shut the door behind him.

Nicely done if I do say so myself. I check the time. About half-two. Mrs O'Shea's at bingo with the rest of the local coffin-dodgers. David's not expecting me back until after three so I head to the garden and pull up a chair. Get out this morning's copy of The Sun and make the most of the unseasonably warm February weather. Nothing like a bit of fresh air to get the blood flowing. My phone goes. It's Jimmy. He's emailing the survey over within the next hour. That'll get Nick off my back and edges me closer to my windfall. David will ask a few questions but a sale's a sale at the end of the day. He's not going to kick up a fuss. His bonus is tied to our total sales. He needs it as much as I do. Especially with the amount of food his missus must get through.

The survey comes through at four-thirty. I drop Nick a text to let him know.

"Six-fifty?" he fires straight back.

"Yep."

"Nice one." Nick's all business.

I give O'Shea a call and tell her the good news. The old fool's delighted. I tell her I'll get her solicitor to give her a call with the details. I say *her* solicitor, but in reality it's the one I'm telling her to use. He bungs me two hundred notes for every deal I push his way. Asks no questions. That's the thing about the property business, once you've convinced the seller to accept a certain price, everyone else is out to make their cut. No one gives a shit about some poor old dear on her own.

I celebrate with a cheeky look at some better apartments in Marbella. Three stars. Practically VIP. If I can push through a couple of these deals I might shout the boys to some plusher digs. Maybe even a villa. If I pull that out the bag I'll be a legend. Well, even more of a legend than I am already.

Chapter Sixteen

"Let's eat in tonight," Amy says as we get to Nando's, "I've got some stuff to show you."

I'm not a fan of change to our Friday night routine. If it's not broken don't fix it has always worked pretty well for me. I eye her suspiciously as the numpty on the door takes us to our table and asks us if we've ever been to Nando's before. Like we've been living under a rock for the last ten years or something.

The fact we're ordering the usual order but eating in throws Pieter on the till somewhat, and the bell-end forgets the Perinaise. I head back over to the till once our food's turned up and linger around while he serves a teenage, white, Rastafarian loser. He realises what he's done as soon as he sees me hanging around, mainly because he does it all the fucking time.

I sit back down at the table, fully Perinaised-up, to find Amy with various print outs stacked in front of her. She passes me one as I'm in the process of taking the first bite out of my chicken burger. It's some kind of apartment. "This one's in Tenerife," she says, "nothing fancy, just cheap and cheerful."

I'm a bit confused, partly because Pieter also forgot the extra order of halloumi with my chicken burger, but mainly because I'm not sure why Amy is passing me various sheets of paper with foreign apartment buildings on them. "For our holiday," she says, reading the uncertainty written all over my face as I stare blankly at another print out; a three star hotel in Gran Canaria.

Shit. She actually thinks we're going to go away together. I scrabble around for the right words. I need to let her down gently. Can't have her making a scene in Nando's.

"Thing is," I say, "me and the lads have been talking." I can already see by the look on her face, like Pieter's given her a Lemon and Herb shite-burger by mistake, that she knows where I'm going with this. There's no other way to say it, so I come straight out with it. "We're going to do a boys' holiday. To Marbella."

"Oh," is all she says. She starts stacking up the print-outs. I've no reason to, because Amy's not my girlfriend and I can bloody well go on holiday with whoever I want and being on tour with the lads will be fucking great banter, but I feel kind of bad, looking at her as she puts all her print-outs back in a folder she's clearly bought just for this. It's even got a sticker on the front. It says *our first holiday*.

"Maybe we could go away in a few months," I say, in an effort to cheer her up.

"It's fine," she replies, "I'm just embarrassed that's all."

"Don't be embarrassed," I say, caring-like, "it's a lovely idea. It's just not the right time for me. I've got a lot going on at work and it's been ages since the lads have all been away together."

"It's fine," she says, again. She clears her throat, takes a deep breath. "So how are the lads?"

Phew. Crisis averted.

I tell her all about Charlie. Tell her he's changed. How I'm worried about him. How I feel like we're drifting apart.

"Maybe he's grown up a bit," she says, the cheeky bitch.

Amy's not her normal energetic self when we get back to the flat. We're lying back on my bed but she's subdued. There are no advances and no wandering hands. She removes her underwear as if it's a chore, and makes no attempt to release me from mine. I do it myself. I put my hand on her thigh to test the waters but she doesn't respond. She doesn't stop me or move away, but she doesn't exactly show much excitement. We skip the foreplay and head straight to the main event. After all, how am I supposed to reciprocate if she doesn't do her part first?

For the first time since we met all those months ago, the sex is functional and joyless, devoid of any enthusiasm from her side. She's unusually selfish and just lies back and expects me to do all the work. I try to work out what's wrong with her as I take charge before we lose all momentum and the night ends in a damp squib. She's unusually quiet. Normally by this point she's writhing around but this evening she's rooted to the spot. Her hands, normally gripping onto my arms and torso, remain resolutely by her sides. She's still enjoying it, obviously, but it's like her hearts not in it.

I up the tempo with no discernible effect. The ridiculous notion occurs to me that perhaps I'm losing my touch, but it quickly vanishes when I recall Michelle's shuddering orgasms and shaking legs from Tuesday night. No, the problem here is Amy, and it's beginning to piss me off. Why bother coming round if you aren't interested in having a good time? A rubbish shag is better than no shag at all, certainly, but it makes bringing things to a conclusion all the more difficult. This is about as erotic as a trip to the dentist.

I turn her over and without her bored face in my eye line I am able to replace her with thoughts of some of my previous antics. My mind wanders back to Michelle's sexual gymnastics. I don't reckon she'd ever turn in such a disappointing performance. Sophie's angry revenge sex from a couple of weeks back crosses my mind. Her transformation from bashful victim to cathartic minx was quite an experience. Maybe I binned her off too soon. I imagine the flailing limbs of the waitress from TGI Fridays from before Christmas. She had absolutely no boundaries. Fantastic. I settle back on imagining Michelle's toned, spray-tanned frame and fantastic jugs. That does the trick.

We lie on the barely ruffled duvet afterwards and catch our breath. I go to offer one of my customary post-sex quips, a one-liner to break the ice, but catch myself. It doesn't seem appropriate. The silence looms in the half-light of my bedroom. I get up and pad across to the bathroom just to escape the atmosphere. I splash cold water on my reddened face to cool off and try to suppress my rising anger. What the fuck is wrong with her? She was fine earlier this evening. I know she was a bit pissy about the talk of me going to Marbella with the lads, but that's why I put my arm around her on the way home. In public. She should know that's a big deal.

I take a couple of deep breaths and head back across the hall. The ominous hush hits me as I close the door behind me. Amy's under the covers now, lying with her back to the door, facing the wall. I watch her shoulders move in time with her breathing for a few seconds before I slide into the bed beside her. She doesn't stir or acknowledge me. I decide silence is the best option and leave her to her mood. She probably just needs to sleep it off. I turn the lamp off and plunge the room into darkness. I stare at the ceiling and let my breathing slow as I wait for the outline of my room to come into focus as my eyes adjust to the blackness.

"Are we ever going to be together properly?" Amy whispers in a resigned tone. The words pierce the silence and hang in the gloom. I leave them there and pretend to be asleep.

Chapter Seventeen

Amy's got her sports bra on and is halfway through the process of pulling her skinny jeans over that delicious rump of hers by the time I open my eyes. I can tell she's still got a cob on from last night by the fact she's not woken me up for a bit of morning action. Not even a fumble. Unusual. She's normally very much a morning person. It's only just gone seven. She's got until about half-nine before I ideally like her to be out of the flat, so fuck knows what she's playing at getting up this early.

She sees me watching her pull on her socks but turns away in silence. The heavy atmosphere hasn't cleared overnight. Amy isn't normally like this. Maybe she's on the blob? I mentally check the date. That can't be it. It's only the twentieth and Amy normally comes on around the twenty-fifth. I know this because that's the weekend I try to avoid her each month. Shitty mood and no sex? You're alright thanks.

She sits on the end of the bed to do up her tatty Converse and begins throwing her last few items into her overnight bag with the kind of force that people use when they want you to know they're pissed off. She wants a reaction. I don't give her the satisfaction. I opt instead to poke her playfully with my foot. See if I can ease her out of it. And back into bed.

It does not have the desired effect.

"How long have I been coming here Danny?" she fires at me. I see real venom in her eyes for the first time. It's a bit unsettling. Maybe she's come on early this month. Apparently sometimes that happens with stress.

I decide damage limitation may be a better strategy, although quite what caused the damage god knows. "Six months or so?" I offer. It's a question more than an answer. I'm honestly not sure. I'm not the sort of bloke who keeps count of that sort of thing. It's not the response she's looking for.

"Try a year. A whole fucking year we've been *seeing each other*, or whatever you want to call it. Last night was a year to the day since our first date."

Christ. What does she want, a fucking anniversary present or something? If that's what she's after then she's barking up the wrong tree and she knows it. "We've been over this," I say as defensively as I dare.

"You're fucking right we have," she shouts. I try to remember if I've ever heard her swear before this morning. I haven't. She normally uses words like *bloomin'* or *bloody* if she's really fuming.

"But you don't want to be *labelled* do you? You don't want to *ruin what we've got.* You won't go away with me, you won't meet my friends. The only reason I've met Chris is because you live with him. The only time we spend together is in your flat or Nando's. You're a piss-taker Danny. I'm just a fuck-buddy to you and you've strung me along for a whole year."

I try to offer some resistance. Some string of words that denies her claim but doesn't push the conversation on any further. Nothing comes to mind. I simply open and close my mouth a couple of times like a goldfish gasping its last breath. The silence pushes her over the edge.

"Fuck you Danny, you're a coward and an arsehole. I'll get out of your hair and leave you to your precious lads' day."

She slams the bedroom door on her way out. Christ. Fucking women and their hormones. I don't know what her problem is. She's bang out of order. She knows how important Saturday with the lads is. It's a tradition.

Amy's outburst has knocked my schedule well off kilter. I try to go back to sleep until my 9:30 alarm goes off but her tone has really got under my skin. I think of line after clever line I could have come out with. I consider texting her a couple of them, but despite my annoyance I decide it wouldn't be a wise move.

I get up and make myself a coffee before taking my regular place in front of Sky Sports. I realise Soccer AM hasn't even started yet, so Christ knows what I'm supposed to watch. I flick the channels past some southern hemisphere slack-jawed cavemen playing rugby and some posh in-bred wankers sailing some boats about. I settle on a random tennis match on Eurosport. One of the women playing is vaguely passable and her skirt is just short enough to show off a bit of cheek when she serves. This is the first positive this morning so far.

Once I've done my coffee I have an hour to wait before I can eat my porridge. I need to eat it exactly one hour before I do my first rep at the gym. I kill the time by playing a game of FIFA. Chris's Playstation is one of the few perks of having him in the flat. I get soundly beaten by an eleven year old from Liverpool. He laughs at me as he scores his sixth in the final minute. I reclaim the high ground by calling his mother a *scouse whore*. Despite being impressed by his extensive vocabulary I turn the game off midway through his rabid response. Finally the clock reaches half nine and my schedule can begin properly.

The porridge, with two added scoops of whey protein and topped with two bananas goes down at 9:30 on the dot. I put away another coffee straight after to get my metabolism up. By the time I meet

Charlie and Gaz outside the gym at 10:15 I'm amped up and ready to put the work in. We smash out a load of reps on the bench press together. Gaz is a big lump and I nearly do my back in trying to keep up with him. Charlie struggles to even get close. He's slacked off a bit recently and is paying the price. If he's not careful his pecs will end up like the tits on one of the old birds hogging the cross-trainers. He ignores our jibes. Seems he's had a bit of a banter bypass this morning.

We always follow up our sesh with a bit of a sauna, to drain a bit of water out of the system. It's the best way to get as lean as possible before a night out. Unfortunately this means having to brush past the congregation of old men who feel the need to walk around the changing rooms air-drying their cocks, but we edge our way past and make the best of it.

By one we've gone our separate ways until the standard 2:30 meet time down the Clapham North at the top of the high street. The last one to arrive (normally Gaz) gets the beers in. We watch Soccer Saturday with our betting slips on the table in front of us. We sink six beers each and celebrate wildly when a last minute goal for Stoke wins me just shy of two hundred quid. As always, if anyone wins big, the night out is on them, so everyone's a winner. We arrange to meet back at the pub at seven to give us time to go home, shower and change.

Back at the flat I select a classic white shirt, blue jeans and brown shoes combo. The birds lap it up every Saturday night. No doubt we'll end up down Inferno's later, where we'll be knee deep in fanny. Amy's bullshit this morning has fired me up to the point where I know someone's in for a pasting tonight. I pass through the living room on the way back out. Chris has got Jurassic Park 2 paused at beginning while he waits for his pizza to arrive. Fuck's sake. The only Double D's he'll be seeing tonight will be Dinosaurs and Dominos. I head back out to get on it with the lads.

The birds we see out and about are ordinary at best. I see a couple of decent ones but don't seem to make much headway with them. Probably lezzers anyway. I gradually lose the rest of the lads. Gaz and Ritz are hanging around some ropey old birds by the bar. No idea where Ben is. Probably banging some bird in the toilets.

I find myself stumbling around the sticky carpets of Inferno's at around two in the morning. I'm not sure why but I've got the rage tonight. Can feel myself a bit hyped up. Eyeing people. Looking for trouble. It happens sometimes. I feel the pressure building up and just need to blow off a bit of steam.

I bowl around the place and bump into a couple of posh pricks. They haven't got the minerals for a scrap though. Practically shit themselves when I start getting lairy. Back away like I'm some kind of lunatic. One of the doormen comes over to see what the fuss is about. Pegs me as the instigator and tells me to call it a night. I tell him he's a wanker and bundle my way through the exit onto the high street.

I don't know what it is but the whole place seems to be full of arseholes tonight. The queue in Subway is full of them. Posh knobheads from Chelsea slumming it in Clapham. I munch my foot-long outside and wait for the biggest twat of the lot to come outside with his braying girlfriend. She drapes herself all over him as she laughs at his shitty posh-boy jokes. Until I lamp him on the jaw. He goes down like the sack of shit that he is. She screams and starts crying while he lies there looking like he's going to piss his pants. I feel better. No need to carry on. No need to put the boot in any further. I turn around and head home, still tucking into my Subway. No one says anything. They haven't got the balls.

Chapter Eighteen

Monday doesn't get off to a good start. Jonty Stresshead comes in at ten to talk about his student flat. I tell him I still think the best he can hope for is four-hundred. He doesn't take it very well. Starts getting proper angry. Calling me a dodgy con-artist. I try to calm him down by telling him I've worked this area for years. That I know the value of a bloody two bedroom flat. He's still raging. Keeps saying I'm cheating him.

David comes over to see what the fuss is about. Jonty reckons he spoke to three other agents over the last week, all of which said they could get him four-eighty at least, maybe five-hundred. A couple of them even had the balls to say they'd heard I sold stuff on the cheap to my mates and that he should steer well clear of me. David steps in and manages to get him to lower his voice. Tells him it must just be a mistake on my part. An honest mistake. I play along. Tell him David's right and apologise. He calms down enough not to smash the place up, which I thought likely when he first walked in. He still storms out though, calling us thieving bastards as he slams the door.

The rest of the office gawp at me like I'm standing there with my pants down. Especially Alice the gormless twat. David pulls me to one side and asks me straight if I was pulling a fast one. If I'd earmarked it for one of my investors. I deny it of course. Tell him what I told Stresshead. It was all a complete misunderstanding. Just a mistake on my part. I can tell David doesn't believe me anymore than Stresshead, but what's he going to do? Go through my phone and check my texts and emails? He hasn't got the balls for that. I head back to my desk, feeling everyone's eyes still on me. I sit down and delete my texts and emails as quickly as possible.

I go for a walk down the high street at lunch and give Amy a call. I need to vent about this morning but she doesn't pick up. The moody cow's probably still in a stress with me after the weekend. She better get over it by Friday. I'm already counting down the days until a Nando's and movie night. I'm still a bit wound up by the time I've picked up a sandwich and bottle of Pepsi Max from Tesco Express. I need some light relief. In a situation like this, there's someone I know I can always turn to; Ellie.

Ellie and me go way back. We met at the gym about five years ago. She was a tall, blonde personal trainer with rock hard abs, year-round tan and a great arse. I booked a few PT sessions with her, which was a bit of a joke considering how ripped I was at the time, but it was the easiest way to get close to her.

I could tell she was up for it straight away. And not looking for anything serious either. Perfect. No hassling me after a couple of dates, wondering where it was all going, asking whether I was seeing other people, giving me GBH of the ears about every little thing. When she told me she'd been single for seven years on our first date I knew I was onto a winner. She wasn't going to be jumping into anything serious anytime soon, she was far too used to being single. Too busy drinking Prosecco with the girls and all that bollocks to want a boyfriend. We went out for a drink, on a Tuesday, and ended up back at mine. She was a sight to behold with her kit off.

After a few weeks we stopped bothering with the charade of going out on dates and just met up at my place for a shag and a movie every few weeks. It's been that way ever since. On average I reckon I doink her at least six times a year. Ellie's a top girl. Low maintenance. We can spend all night going to town on each other, go our separate ways, and it's often months before one of us even thinks about getting in touch.

I drop her a text when I get back into the office to see what she's up to this week. An evening with Ellie is just what I need with all this stress at work and grief I'm getting from Amy.

"Hello stranger," she fires straight back. Within ten minutes she's sending me pictures of herself in her underwear. We arrange for her to come over on Thursday. What a girl. I can always rely on Ellie.

I get back to a silent flat after work. There's no geeky film playing on the TV. No depressing music wafting out of Chris's room. I can't remember the last time the flat was this empty and quiet. The silence is unsettling. My first thought is that something bad has happened. Maybe Chris has finally realised the pointlessness of his existence and done something about it. The horrifying possibility that I'll have to advertise for another flat mate occurs to me. It's just such a total ball-ache.

I'm just about to go into his room to check he hasn't keeled over from an asphixiwank gone wrong or something when the front door goes and he practically crawls through the door, as red as a phone box. He's got some huge tent of a t-shirt on, with sweat rings around what can only be describes as his tits. It's an old t-shirt, faded, with 'Just Do It' emblazoned across the front. It looks like he's just done it and given himself a heart attack. On his feet he's got some battered reeboks. The daft prick's only been for a run. Fair play to him, I wouldn't be seen dead running down the street with tits like that bouncing around. I'm amazed he hasn't got a pair of black eyes.

"Fucking hell, mate," I say. "Are you alright?"

He nods as he's greedily sucking in the air, like it's a half-price stuffed crust pizza, desperately trying to get his breath back.

"It's been a while," he manages to gasp, before heading into the kitchen and pounding a pint of water. He sees me staring at him, amused. "I don't want to be a fat fucker anymore," he says. Fair enough. I can't argue with that.

He does himself a kale and spinach smoothie for dinner. Nothing else. He must be starving. I give this bollocks two days at the most.

He'll be shoving a pizza down his throat by Thursday night. I make myself a big plate of fish-fingers, waffles and beans and make a point of eating it right in front of him while he scoops out the dregs of his smoothie with a spoon. I give Amy another call. She doesn't answer. Fuck her then.

Chapter Nineteen

Ellie arrives bang on seven on Thursday night. Tight vest top and no bra. One of my favourite looks. Comfy jeans, slung low with her yellow thong poking above the waistband. There's no pretence with Ellie. She doesn't dress to impress. She just wants to get her gear off as soon as possible. Her hair's tied up in a bun. She means business. I hope for Chris's sake he's got some earplugs for tonight. We head straight to the bedroom. "Put on Donnie Brasco," she says, which is a bit of a running joke. We've started watching it at least twenty times since we first met but neither of us have any idea what happens after the first half an hour. By the time I've put the DVD in the machine she's whipped off her vest top and jeans, with only a thong remaining. It contrasts nicely with her freshly applied tan. I don't even bother pressing play.

It's been three months since I've seen Ellie but we're so used to each other we pick straight up where we left off. She's in even better condition than the last time I saw her. She's been training hard and putting her workout pictures up on Instagram the last few months. She's built quite a following. Mainly because she looks incredible.

She knows it too, as she spends the whole time we're boning watching herself in the mirror. Tremendous. The other thing I love about Ellie is that she's totally uninterested in staying over. She's in the gym at six-thirty every morning so she makes her excuses and leaves as soon as she's had enough action. She just pulls her clothes on, gives me a wink and heads to the door. I don't even need to get up and show her out.

As soon as Ellie's gone I message Amy. It's been nearly a week now since I heard from her. I assume she's still coming over tomorrow night but she's pushing her luck. If she carries on being like this I'll have to bump her for somebody else.

*****

Six-thirty comes and goes on Friday and I still haven't heard from Amy. I try her again one last time just before seven, but it goes straight to voicemail. I guess Nando's and a movie is off the table tonight. Maybe she's still on her period or whatever, but not to let me know she's not coming is just fucking rude. I got home early tonight to tidy the place up a bit. I didn't go to the gym or arrange something else just in case she did turn up, which pisses me off. I could have had another bird over if I'd known I was going to be on my own twiddling my thumbs.

"Fancy a Nando's?" I say to Chris. I don't see why I should miss out on my usual Friday night treat just because Amy is being a stroppy bitch. He looks at me like I've just offered him half of my lottery winnings. He can't say yes fast enough.

"Tell you what," I say, "I'll go and grab the food and you choose a movie to put on." The loser's practically got a boner.

"Awesome," he manages to spit out after a couple of stuttering false starts, "is Amy coming over?"

"No," I say, "not tonight." I leave before the muppet starts questioning me any further.

Pieter at Nando's doesn't recognise me. What a prick. I come here every fucking week. I have to sit down next to a teenage couple for ten minutes while I wait for the food. I can't not stare at them, simply because she takes up about eighty percent of my field of vision. She is colossal. A real whale. One of those big Goth types with weird pink extensions and a black tent of a dress on. He's a skinny little runt with blue streaks in his hair. I'm sure he tells her that beauty is all about what's inside and all that bollocks, when in reality she's the only one desperate enough to let him put his bony hands all over her. They're disgusting. I decide to wait by the counter in case I catch something off their clothes.

The bloke in the off license recognises me at least. "No pretty lady tonight?" he asks as I hand over the money for the beers and whisky I'm already gagging to get stuck into.

"No, not tonight," I say. Jesus fucking Christ, all anyone ever mentions is bloody Amy.

Chris has got Jurassic Park 3 ready to go when I get back. More fucking dinosaurs. He really is a total loser. He devours the chicken burger in record time while I ask him about Anna. He doesn't burst into tears at the mention of her name, which is a step forward from a month ago. He even shrugs it off when I point out how fit she was.

"Yeah, she was," he says wistfully, "but you know, I can't force her to like me can I? I just have to accept that it's over." Christ. Did Dale Winton here turn into Gandhi while I was out getting the chicken?

"Someone that decent doesn't come along very often though do they?" I say, really trying to ram the point home.

"I was thinking," he says, ignoring my jibe, "maybe it's time I got out there again. Maybe started dating again. I'm not going to meet someone else sitting in here am I?"

"Hold the fucking phone Chris," I say, "are you telling me that you're ready to stop being a Billy-mopey-bollocks and actually step into the outside world again?"

He nods hesitantly. I can see the thought still scares him, but he's reached a tipping point. Frantically wanking himself to sleep every night over the memories of the girl who broke his heart just doesn't cut it anymore. His need for new stimulus has taken control of his fear. He's ready to get out of his comfort zone. Anything to move on and feel the buzz of potential love again. Or in his case heartbreak. At least it'll be new though.

I actually can't wait to hear about all the appalling dates he's going to go on. About all the girls he meets that aren't going to call him back. I invite him on the boys' night we've got planned for a couple of weeks' time as well, which will be absolutely classic. The boys will absolutely eat him alive. There's no way the fat lump is ready for their level of banter.

Chapter Twenty

I'm up early doors on Saturday morning. Me and Gaz have tickets for Chelsea. Home to Spurs, FA Cup quarter-final. Games against that lot are always tasty, both in the stands and on the pitch. It's a lunchtime kick-off so we need to get cracking if we're going to fit in a few beers beforehand. I give Amy another call once I'm out the shower but it goes straight to voicemail. This silent treatment is doing my nut in. It's not eight o'clock yet so maybe she's not up yet to be fair to her.

I meet Gaz at West Brompton tube at ten-thirty and we head down to The Goose for a couple of pints to get the blood pumping. Always a load of Chelsea knocking around here before kick-off and the Stellas aren't as pricey as the pubs closer to the ground. We sink a couple of pints and start walking down towards The Bridge, joining up with a few other lads walking the same way. We manage to fit in a couple of cans each on the walk down there. There's a right good atmosphere in the ground before kick-off. Tottenham's a Jewish club so we do a few songs about the gas chambers, to get the banter going. All part of the game.

The game's a bad tempered one, loads of fouls, players squaring up to each other, that sort of thing. We do our best to get under the skin of their players and it seems to do the trick. Their left-back, Danny Rose's a black fella and we give him a shedload of stick the whole second half. A few songs about slavery, a few monkey chants. One of the older lads chucks a banana at him. Classic. He ends up getting sent off and gives us lot the finger as he walks off the pitch. Fucking liberty. A couple of the lads have to be held back from trying to get on the pitch to have a go at him. Fucking millionaire cry-babies the lot of them. If you can't take a bit of banter from the stands and stay professional then you shouldn't be getting all that money. We do them two-nil. I like to think we did our part.

We see a few spurs fans on the bus home and have a bit of a scuffle with them. One of them gets a few good digs in but like their team, they come off second best. The bus driver chucks us all off the bus and calls the pigs so we have to leg it. A fucking great day all in all.

I've got a right hangover on Sunday. All day boozing does that to me these days. I just can't put it away like I used to. My mum calls but I ignore it. I can't face her grilling me today. I call Amy a few times, but she's still not picking up. I leave a message asking her what's going on. As much as spending last Friday night with my loser flatmate wasn't quite as bad as I expected, it is not an experience I'm keen on making a habit of, and if Amy is intent on carrying on with this moody bitch act, then I'll just have to cut her out for a while and roll someone else in. We'll see how she likes being on the receiving end.

I mentally go through my options. Ellie's the obvious candidate for promotion to the vacant Friday night slot. Banging body, decent face, low maintenance, monster appetite in the sack. Michelle's probably next in line but she's been a bit needy on the texting over the last week so I might have to keep her waiting for a couple more weeks. Giving her a Friday night slot would send her the wrong message. I didn't reply to her last text a few days ago either, so I may have to do a bit of work to get her back onside anyway. I've always got Emma from school if I'm really struggling. I'll try Ellie first. She sent me a picture of herself in the shower yesterday so she shouldn't take much persuading.

I may as well work in a call centre Monday and Tuesday are so shit. All I do is chase Mrs O'Shea's solicitor to check he's got everything he needs to get moving, and field calls from people desperate to get a look at Mrs Baker's place. Its half term and I'd rather not do a load of viewings while she's got a kid hanging off each tit, so I stack them all up for Friday, when she'll be out with the kids visiting her parents for the day.

David's all over me as usual. Wanting to see all the paperwork about the O'Shea sale. He's suspicious, but we've used my mate loads before, he does proper surveys for us as well, so the prick won't find anything.

Nick calls me for an update. I tell him it's all in hand. He also wants to know what's happening with Jonty Stresshead's flat but I have to tell him it's a no-go. I don't tell him that the posh dickhead managed to work out I was trying to screw him over in case he thinks I'm losing my touch. Nick sounds pissed off. He can be a greedy fucker sometimes. Looks like I'll have to wait a bit until I speak to him about upping my commission. I have a quick look online and see Stresshead's flat's on with Foxtons. They've got it on for five-hundred grand. Fucking Foxtons. Bunch of jumped up little pricks with their wanker cars.

I give Ellie a call about Friday. The dozy bint doesn't realise she's been upgraded to a prime weekend slot at first, and starts banging on about her training early on Saturday morning. She's not the brightest sometimes. Good job she's so fit or she'd never get anywhere in life. She caves eventually when I offer her to buy her a Nando's.

"Oooh," she says, "I've never had a Nando's before."

I try to imagine how that is even possible.

Chapter Twenty-One

Chris is out running again on Friday morning before work. I have to hand it to the dickhead, he's really putting the work in. That's every morning this week he's been out pounding the streets. No doubt he'll be ruining it with his customary Friday night pizza tonight though.

Charlie and Alice are both off today so there's no lunchtime banter and beers with him to break up the day. Just wave after wave of cretins pretending they can afford the Baker house. It's been getting a lot of interest, so hopefully we'll get it sold pretty sharpish. It's just me and David in the office all day, so I make sure I spend as much time outside as possible. Luckily I've pretty much got back to back viewings all day so I don't have to interact with the arsehole too much.

Those fuckwits Marcus and Jo-Jo are my first viewing of the day. The place is on at five-hundred grand for fuck's sake. They must earn forty thousand between them, tops. Unless they've won the lottery this is a colossal waste of everyone's time.

"What's your budget?" I ask as I greet them at the front door. I'm not really in the mood for pleasantries.

Marcus stutters a bit. A tell-tale sign of incoming bullshit. "Around four-fifty," he says. He even blushes when he says its. I bet he's shit at poker.

Jo-Jo waltzes into the kitchen and starts banging on about all the dinner parties she'd be able to host here. I cut her off before she gets a chance to really get going. "Do you have mortgage offer in place?" I ask, as pointedly as possible. I can't really be arsed with this whole charade today.

"Well, no, not yet," says Marcus. He's really stuttering now. Like he's doing Scatman John at the karaoke. Jo-Jo's finally shut her cake-hole as well.

"So how do you know what your budget is?" I ask.

"Well, I guess we don't," he finally admits after another bout of stuttering.

"Ok," I say, as arsily as possible, "let's do some back-of-fag-packet calculations shall we? How much do you two earn together, ball-park?"

He hesitates, "About fifty thousand," he says, which probably means it's nearer forty, but I let it slide.

"Deposit?"

"We've saved up about eight thousand over the last couple of years," he says, quietly. He knows the games up.

"Ok then, well the best lender out there will probably give you a mortgage of about two hundred grand. Add that to your measly deposit and you're about three hundred grand short of what you need for this place."

"Oh," says Jo-Jo, who obviously lives in her own fucking world. Marcus, who obviously doesn't, says nothing. I show them the door.

The next viewing doesn't mess about. The bloke oozes money. Bowls up dressed like James Bond, driving a Jag. His wife is clearly the decision maker though. He barely moves from the living room while I'm taking her round the place.

"I love it," she gushes on her way back downstairs. She repeats this for husband, whose checking out the bookshelf in the corner.

"Ok," he says to her, barely looking up from some leather-bound book he's leafing through. He puts it back and shakes my hand firmly. "I'll be in touch," he says, before they head out. They've been and gone in under ten minutes. What a life it must be to casually consider spending half a million quid with the same due diligence I take when I'm buying a packet of Monster Munch.

Unfortunately the rest of the viewings aren't quite as smooth. A neurotic Irish woman takes a good hour and asks every question under the sun. I answer her where I can and bullshit her when I can't. A young couple are keen but they need to sell their flat nearby first, which isn't ideal if I want to tie this up quickly. A couple of birds in their early thirties turn up last. I can't quite work out if they're lezzers or not. One of them's quite fit, in a skinny sort of way. Obviously runs a lot. Lean. I probably would.

They bicker like an old married couple the whole time so I assume they're at least tampering with each other now and again. I give the skinny one my card just in case they're not. Or even better if they are but need an extra pair of hands in the mix. The other one glares at me. They must be at it.

David's in a good mood when I get back because he's just booked his summer holiday in Torremolinos. Although why he's looking forward to spending a whole week with his whale of a wife and their two minging kids I'm not sure. I'm pretty sure one of them is retarded in some way. He nearly cracks a boner when I tell him I expect at least a couple of the viewings to put in an offer on the Baker place. He even asks me if I want a quick drink down the pub after work. I tell him I've got plans and I'm out the door on the dot of five. "Have a good weekend," calls David after me. I don't answer him.

The evening does not get off to a great start. It's gone seven by the time Ellie arrives, despite the fact I specifically told her to be here at six-thirty. Amy was never late. Chris notices that the girl at the door with the overnight bag is not Amy and looks at me like he's just smelt a bad fart. He ejects the Hunger Games DVD he's cued up to start, and takes it into his room. He makes some kind of face at me when he comes back for the chicken salad he's made for his dinner. I ignore him. He can wank himself into oblivion watching Katniss Everdeen for all I care.

Ellie, of course, doesn't notice the change in atmosphere. She's checking her abs in the living room mirror. They look immense. She catches me looking at them and grins. She's going to end up being marched straight into the bedroom if she's not careful, and end up missing out on her first Nando's experience. I tear her away from her reflection and bundle her out of the front door. I need to eat soon or I'll start getting pissed off. Amy always used to take the piss out of me for getting moody when I was hungry.

I notice something that's never occurred to me before when we get to Nando's; Ellie is pretty fucking stupid. I have to step in and do the order when Pieter has to explain the food options to her three times. At one point I think he's really going to lose his rag. She has a plain chicken breast, corn on the cob and coleslaw. It is the single most boring order in the history of Nando's. We make our way to the off-license, which proves to be a bit pointless from Ellie's point of view, as she reveals she's not drinking this month, due to some kind of weight-cutting cycle she's on. She begins going into more detail but my eyes glaze over.

"Better make it eight Stellas tonight boss," I say to the guy behind the counter while she's still rattling on. I get a bottle of wine as well, just to be sure I don't run out of alcohol.

I unpack the food at home and she spends a good five minutes taking photos of it for her Instagram feed. "I need to show my followers what's I'm eating," she says. I'm not convinced that anyone could possible give a shit that she's eating Nando's tonight, but I'm proved wrong by the number of people that relentlessly comment on her pictures while I'm selecting a film to watch. She's delighted by the response. Over a hundred likes in five minutes.

"I don't really like Will Ferrell," she says, as I offer her a few movie options. I look at her, incredulous. Who doesn't like Will Ferrell? Someone with shit banter that's who. She turns her nose up at Superbad as well, saying something about it being 'boy humour'. I assumed from the fact Amy liked all of the same movies as me that they appealed to everyone. Obviously not. "How about something like James Bond?" she asks, oblivious to the fact that liking James Bond makes her a total fucking cretin.

"James Bond? What are you, fifty?" I say. She looks at me blankly. "Shall we just go for Donnie Brasco?" I ask. It's only just gone eight o'clock but I can't face much more talking.

Mercifully she agrees and we head straight for the bedroom. All thoughts of how annoying she is disappear when Ellie whips her clothes off. She is a fucking knockout. It occurs to me that Chris would kill his entire family for the opportunity to be in this position, with a naked Ellie within touching distance. I resolve to make the best of it. As loudly as possible.

We manage to keep the chat to a minimum until about eleven when she feels it necessary to fill the heaving, sweaty silence with some more inane chatter about her lifelong dream to go to Australia. I humour her, mainly because I'm too knackered to be pedantic. "Oh right," I say. "When do you think that'll be?"

"Two weeks tomorrow. I booked my flights yesterday. I'm so excited."

"What?" I say, a bit too sharply. This was not part of the plan. Ellie was my fall back option. My Plan B. She's been banging on about going there for the last five years. I never thought she'd actually do it.

"Oh," she says, "Sorry, I didn't think. You aren't upset are you?"

Upset. UPSET. Don't make me laugh. "No of course not," I say, "I always knew you'd go eventually," I lie. I didn't really. I honestly thought she'd end up an old lady stuck in a home somewhere, bending the ears of the orderlies about wanting to go to Australia while they cleaned out her bedpan. It's not upsetting. It's just annoying. Purely from a logistical point of view.

She nuzzles in close to me, whispering how sorry she is. About how we can make the most of the next couple of weeks, maybe watch Donnie Brasco a few times. A mild panic rises somewhere inside me as I realise the holes now appearing in my dating schedule. I need to put some effort in. Replenish the stocks. I wait until she's drifted off to sleep and get out my phone to fire out a few lines. See if I get anything back.

"Fuck off you wanker" is Sophie's simple response. I laugh. Fair enough. I did completely pie her off after all. She didn't ignore me though, so maybe there's room for manoeuvre on that one. I get a more positive response from Michelle. A simple 'hello you, I was hoping you'd get back in touch". I can pencil her in then. I toy with the idea of messaging Amy, but decide against it. She needs to show a bit of humility before I get in touch with her again.

Chapter Twenty-two

Ellie's up early Saturday morning as she's got a client to train at eight. I give her one for the road. She watches us in the mirror. I say 'us' but she's pretty focused on herself. Sometimes I wonder if she even notices I'm there. But if she's off to Australia in a couple of weeks I'd better make the most of it before some antipodean animal gets his filthy surfer hands all over her. She takes a few pictures of herself in the mirror afterwards. In her thong and sports bra. Apparently, when you first wake up is the best time to show off your abs, as that's when you're at your most dehydrated. She needs to update her Instagram community she says.

I suspect her Instagram community is ninety percent teenage boys wanking into their gym socks, and ten percent fat girls wishing they look like her but I don't want that to be the last time I shag her so I don't say anything. The fact Ellie barely eats any carbs and trains twice a day, six days a week, and is relentlessly putting away protein shakes doesn't seem to be mentioned an awful lot to her band of followers. I suspect that's to stop the *community* realising you need to do more than walk on a treadmill twice a week to look like she does. She gives a little wiggle of her bum and leaves me in bed as she heads off for the gym.

I turn my phone on. I pick up the conversation with Michelle from last night. I lie and tell her I'm away this weekend, but suggest meeting up sometime next week. She practically salivates. It's a bit pathetic really. I fire up Tinder while I'm sitting on the toilet, and match with a few girls. I can barely be arsed but I send a few messages anyway. There's nothing on there that gets my blood pumping. Better make sure I bag a decent bird out tonight with the lads. I need to start restocking the shelves.

I meet Gaz at the gym. Charlie's not with him. He's at work instead, trying to tie up another deal apparently. He's relentless at the moment. Still won't do him any good though. That end of year bonus is mine. Gaz reckons he's not coming out with the boys tonight either. Says he's not feeling great and needs a quiet one. I'm really starting to wonder what's going on with him. Charlie's been my best mate the last few years, since I moved to the area. He told me all about his past. About his ex. About all the things he wanted to put behind him. He's the only one I confided in about my small issue with the law back in the day as well. Just to make sure he knew we both had things we wanted to forget about, and that we could trust each other. But lately he's been quiet. Like he's pulled back a bit from the lads. From me. He probably just needs a shag. God knows it's been a few weeks.

Gaz and me smash out a good session on the weights. We need to up the workload if we're going to be in top condition by the time we hit Marbs. We spot a couple of fit girls on their own at the squat rack. They've got all the gear. Coloured leggings practically spray-painted to their arses. Little vests barely covering sports bras that push their tits up to their chins. Don't reckon they've been doing weights too long as their arse-cheeks have still got a bit of give to them by the looks of it. Not like the carved-from-stone look Ellie's got going on.

"You need to be careful with your form," I say to the little one with the bright yellow leggings, "you'll do your back in squatting like that."

They give us the once over, but their fear of being chatted up in the gym wavers when they see the size of Gaz's biceps and how ripped my chest is at the moment. Situations like this are the precise reason I wear muscle vests at the gym. The one I've got on today barely covers my nipples, let alone my chest. The little one tries unsuccessfully not to gawp.

"Can you give us any tips then?" asks the other one, a lean blonde decked out in all-matching Nike kit.

I smile at her. "No problem," I say. I stand behind the little one with one hand on the small of her back and one on her stomach, which is pleasingly flat and toned. I squat down with her slowly, telling her to push her bum out more and straighten her back. "Really engage your core," I hear myself say whilst somehow keeping a straight face. The girls absolutely lap it up. We tell them we're just heading down to the sauna and hot tub if they want to join us. Obviously they do.

The small one introduces herself as Jess while we're soaking up the bubbles. I'm pleased to see she looks just as good in her bikini as in her gym kit. It turns out it's not the sports bra that gives her an insane rack. That's just nature. We don't hang around long. The football starts in an hour and we're meeting Ritz down the pub. I make sure to let Jess know where we're heading tonight. She's got definite potential.

Soccer Saturday is already on in the pub when we arrive. Ritz and Ben have already commandeered our regular table in front of the big screen and got the beers in. Ritz's wearing his Pompey shirt today and clutching his betting slip. He's got twenty notes on a Portsmouth, Crewe, Birmingham and Arsenal accumulator. All away from home. Thirty-five to one. He always sticks Pompey in his bets, the mug. Blinded by loyalty. They've got no chance today, away at high-flying Burton Albion.

We sink the first pints within ten minutes. Arsenal are already one up. They should be a banker. I've got them in a treble with Palace and West Ham. Gaz has got some daft first goal scorer bets on. He never wins. He may as well be throwing his money down the road every week. Ben never gets too involved in the gambling side of things.

Midway through the second pint Arsenal score again. They'll be out of sight by half time. Palace and West Ham are both losing, which means my bet is pretty much sunk already. Ritz is getting nervous now. Crewe and Birmingham are both one up as well. He just needs his beloved Pompey to come up with the goods and he'll be quids in. Unfortunately they're shit. They concede on the stroke of half time and he stomps off to the bar to get some more beers in. It's not his round but we aren't complaining. Ben's chatting up some old munter at the table next to us as the half-time whistles go. The rest of us have a chat about Charlie in the half-time lull. Ritz reckons he's just having a quiet few weeks but I'm not so sure. There's definitely something up.

"Maybe he's got a bird," pipes up Gaz. Sometimes it takes the mind of a child to cut through the bullshit. It would explain a lot, but surely he'd have told me. We're best mates.

Ritz starts banging on about his car at the start of the second half. He's just fitted a chrome exhaust, which apparently looks wicked. I go to the bar and leave Gaz to listen to him chuffing on. Palace concede again while I'm getting the drinks which completely fucks my bet. No coming back from that now. Gaz's bets have all gone tits up as well, so it's just Ritz and his thirty-five to one job that's in play. Ten minutes to go and his beloved Pompey are still one down. Ritz is gutted and goes to the bar to get a round of Sambucas in. That's the things about gambling. No matter how long the odds, you're already spending the money in your head.

We bang back the shots and Pompey equalise. Hold up, we're back on. Only five minutes left though. We nervously sip our beers. We're nearly all empty but there's no way anyone's going to the bar until this is over. Full time scores start flashing up at the bottom of the screen. Arsenal win. Palace lose. Birmingham win. West Ham draw. Crewe win. Hope fades. Ninety-fourth minute now. Ritz slumps back in his chair. He was already working out what to spend that seven hundred quid on. I start stacking the army of empty glasses in front of us. Pompey score. We go mental. Proper fucking mental. A couple of glasses go over as we jump around in a little huddle, screaming the place down. We sit down, exhausted. What a rush. Charlie will be gutted he missed it. I give him a shout on the way back home while Ritz and Gaz hit the bookies to pick up the winnings.

He doesn't answer but I leave a message to tell him about the big win. We're celebrating tonight I say. Tell him to give me a call back if he changes his mind. Should be a big one.

I have a quick shower and throw on a shirt. I'm a bit pissed so I try Amy again. I leave a message telling her that whatever I've done I'm sorry. That I want to make it up to her. Hopefully she'll know I'm serious. I'm just finishing off a quick can of Stella before I head back out when Chris appears in the living room. He's got shoes and a shirt on. He's even had a shave and a haircut. "Alright if I tag along?" he says.

Fuck me. There's a turn up for the books.

Chapter Twenty-three

"Ping."

"Ping."

"Ping."

"Pong."

Chris hesitates for a fraction. He's not sure. He guesses: "Pong."

Laughter erupts around the table as he realises he's wrong. Again. Unfortunately for someone with his limited exposure to drinking games, a night out with the Wolf Pack involves a lot of them. Inevitably this leads to him downing drink after drink. We try to make it easier by playing the simplest drinking game ever created; 'Ping Pong' but the bell-end can't even get that right.

"You can't Pong a Pong! How are you still getting this wrong?" Ben cries between bouts of laughter. He's right, Chris is completely incapable of learning the most basic of rules.

"*Down it, down it, down it*" chant the rest of the boys as they stand around him while he chews his way through the remainder of his sixth pint. It's only nine o'clock. Fair play to him, he's getting stuck in and taking it all in good spirits. He's done well with the running and eating this week as well, he already looks like he's lost a bit of timber. The haircut and shave have taken about ten years off him as well. Maybe there's hope for him yet. He might even find a bird if he can find one pissed enough. He'll need to learn how to take his drink though. He's already slurring all over the place.

Ritz gets us in all in a huddle. "I got us a surprise," he says, "as we're celebrating tonight." He opens up his palm to reveal a nice little packet of gear. Quality. What a ledge. Tonight's really shaping up to be a big one. I head straight to the cubicles with him for the first line, although judging by his eyes he's had a cheeky go on his way to the pub. He racks them up on the toilet seat and I feel the familiar burn as I do mine. I draw a cock on the cubicle door while Ritz has his go.

I decide it's time to crank things up a notch as we come back to the bar. I get everyone two Sambucas and a pint to kick things on a bit. This place needs to know who the top boys are around here. We take it in turns on the gear. Chris doesn't touch it because he's some kind of woofter. We do the lot in the pub as they sometimes check you on the way into Aquum.

We get in no problem, although Chris is properly smashed by this point. It's only half-nine so Kev on the door gives him the benefit of the doubt. I tell him I'll keep him on water for the next hour or so, to sober him up. Obviously that's a load of bollocks and I stick a vodka in his beer as soon as we get to the bar. He's a bit unsteady on his feet but we're all in the same boat there. He tries to ease off a bit but we give him a bit of peer pressure. He toes the line when we get the next round of Schooners and shots in.

It's just after ten and the place is already packed. I see a tall blonde who stands out a mile. Proper fit. She's making eyes at me. I recognise her from somewhere. Can't quite place her though. I head over and say hello.

"I think I've seen you on Tinder," I say, by way of an opening line.

"No. You definitely haven't," she says. That's killed the conversation. There's an awkward moment while the alcohol jams my brain. I jabber a few sentences out for what feels like an eternity. She looks at me sympathetically. As if maybe she thinks I don't do this sort of thing very often, which makes me hate her. Her mate looks at me like I've just crawled out from under the nearest rock. I make my excuses and leg it. What the hell happened there? Opening on girls is normally a strong point of mine. I need another drink after that shit-show.

I do another shot. The air feels cloudier in here tonight. The lights swim around and everything merges on the periphery of my vision. I wink at another bird further down the bar. I need to put that last effort behind me. She smiles back. Panic over. I've still got it.

Chris is talking to someone by the bar. It takes me a few seconds to realise who it is. It's Amy. I didn't notice her come in. It's been two weeks since she stormed out of my flat. She looks good. Black top and skinny jeans. Nice big heels as well. Her legs and arse look hot. She's made a real effort tonight. I take my eyes off her for a moment and realise there's some bloke standing with her. Some short little runt in a blazer. He's shaking hands with Chris. Looks like Amy's introducing them. Ritz and Gaz come over to me as I'm taking it all in. "Who's that dickhead?" I ask him, nodding my head over at the runt.

"No idea," he says. The bloke's got his hand on her back. A bit too intimate to be a mate. I decide to go over and see what she's playing at, bringing some bloke in here with her. Mugging me off on my own turf.

"Alright Amy," I say. The words are harder to get out than I expected. My tongue feels thicker than normal.

Chris stares at me, a look in his eye I can't quite work out. The other guy gives me daggers. Amy isn't like that, she's more polite. "Hi Danny," she says. "How have you been?"

How have I been? Like we've not seen each other for years. Like I wasn't sticking my knob in her only a couple of weeks back.

"Not bad," I say, but the words don't feel like they're coming out of my mouth. It's like I'm watching someone else. "Phone not working at the moment?"

"I didn't want to speak to you," she says, the atmosphere changing. "I still don't. Let's not do this here, Danny."

"Well where else are we going to fucking do it? You never answer your phone and never call me back?" I don't mean to swear but it just comes out. Makes me sound much more aggressive than I mean to.

The arsehole standing next to her pipes up at this point. "Don't speak to her like that mate," he says, like he's her fucking dad or something.

"Why don't we go and get a drink," says Chris, trying to defuse the situation by herding me towards the bar. I don't know whose side he reckons he's on. I push back past him to the midget prick standing next to Amy.

"Look mate," he says before I can say anything else, stepping in front of Amy as he does it, "she doesn't want to talk to you, so just leave it yeah?"

I'm filled with an overwhelming urge to leather the little weasel.

So I do.

It turns out Amy's new boyfriend is pretty tasty with his hands and the ruck doesn't last very long. I miss with my windmill attempt at a punch and he chins me with a right hand, catches me flush on the jaw. I go down in a heap, because of the alcohol, not the punch. Amy storms off, disgusted by the whole thing. At least that's fucked his chances as well. I pick myself up with the help of Chris and Kev the doorman, who's waddled over to see what all the commotion's about.

"What's going on?" he says. Typical doorman, comes over after all the actions finished.

"Nothing Kev," I say. "Just handbags. The geezer and his slag have left now anyway."

I head back to the bar and get another drink with the lads. I need to push that shit out of my mind, so I sink a few more shots before moving onto the whisky. I'm too bloated from all the beers now anyway. Chris makes his excuses and leaves. Pussy. Ben's pulled some old minger and gone back with her. It's just me, Gaz and Ritz left, pounding back the drinks. Giving it large.

The boys cheer me up, tell me I was well within my rights to hit the bloke. That is was Amy's fault for bringing him in here in the first place. They're right of course. She was bang out of order. We keep throwing the whisky back. I try to chat some birds up. They aren't having any of it. It's full of stuck up bitches in here tonight. The whole place is getting on my tits. I've had enough of it. I just want to go home. Gaz won't let me and hands me a Sambuca. Tells me to man up and stop moaning. I nod. He's right. Plenty more where she came from. I sling back the shot and order another round.

Chapter Twenty-four

I assume someone's performed brain surgery on me during the night, as I wake up with a sharp jolt pulsing through my forehead. The air in the room is soupy and thick, infused with the stale stench of the alcohol that's been seeping through my pores all night. My body's desperate for water but I can't bring myself to move. My mouth feels like it's been chewing on cotton wool all night. I notice how tender my jaw is, and last night's scuffle comes back to me. A warm, flushed feeling of shame creeps across my face. It's been a few years since I've felt that. I wish I could dig a hole in the floor and crawl inside. I'm embarrassed but I can't take it back now. Nothing I can do can turn back the clock. Despite the lads convincing me that I was well within my rights to lamp the bloke, I know the whole thing was my fault. Too much drink and the surprise of seeing Amy with someone else. Ultimately, I behaved like a dickhead. There's not really an excuse I can come up with to justify it, even to myself. I should call her to apologise. I remember heading back to the bar after it all went off, but not much else. I've got no idea how I got home, or how I made it into my room.

There's more banging, this time outside my head. Someone's knocking on the bedroom door. It's Chris, wanting to check I'm alright. It's nearly four o'clock apparently. In the afternoon. That can't be right. I check the time on my phone. Fucking hell, I really have been out for the count.

"I got you a bottle of Lucozade and a Steak slice from Greggs," he says as I emerge from the stale fumes in my room. He gestures to a collection of packages he's left on the coffee table. I could kiss him. The thought of leaving the flat today is a terrifying prospect, and the only thing in the fridge is a half empty tub of Lurpak. It occurs to me that Chris is a decent bloke really. I'm definitely lucky he's around this morning. Maybe it's the emotional turmoil of my rancid hangover, but I also concede to myself that I'm glad he's my flatmate.

I sit down on the sofa opposite him, my eyes blinking in the light like a new born child. "How are you feeling?" he says as I smash down half the Lucozade in one gulp. The angry bubbles fill my throat and make my eyes water. I gasp for air.

"I'm alright." I say when I get my breath back. "No idea how I got home though." I'm trying to make light of it but it's not quite coming off. My voice is flat. Sad even. I feel like maybe I crossed a line last night. I can tell he actually feels sorry for me. That's a turn up for the books. "Is it really four in the afternoon?" I say, moving the subject along.

"Yeah. I heard you come home about four-thirty last night. I could hear you knocking around a bit. There were a few bangs. I thought about coming into check on you but decided against it."

That would explain the reason my TV's hanging off its wall mount this morning then. I'll have a go at sorting that out when my head's cleared a bit. I look at the steak slice he's got me. I tear off a piece of the pastry and force it down. Christ I feel rough. The thought of the steak and gravy sauce sloshing around my mouth makes me want to puke so I save the rest for later on. I sink back into the sofa and close my eyes. We don't discuss the fight. There's an unspoken understanding that I don't want to be reminded of it.

"Have you heard from Amy?" he asks.

"No," I reply. We leave it there.

"I've got some news," Chris pipes up, changing the subject. He's all excited. I open my eyes a touch to hear what he's got to say. "I met a girl last night."

"Oh yeah?" I say, trying not to sound too shocked even though, frankly, it's a fucking miracle.

"Yeah, a girl called Ruby, I met her in the kebab shop after Aquum." Christ. The kebab shop. God knows what she looks like.

He starts jabbering about how he left after the fight because he couldn't face drinking anymore. I call him a lightweight but maybe I should have done the same. He's grinning like a kid on Christmas morning the whole time he's speaking. "I walked in there to get a chicken shish, and there was this girl sitting on her own," he says, "just sitting in the corner. Crying."

"Vulnerable, always a good type," I say, trying to get a bit of banter going, but it comes out all wrong. My voice is flat and I don't have the energy for it this morning. He ignores me and carries on.

"I didn't say anything to her at first. I'm not good at that stuff like you are. The thought of going up to a girl I don't know terrifies me." He says.

"But then this group of lads came in and started hassling her. One of them kept trying to sit next to her to chat her up. It was really upsetting her; she kept crying and telling him to leave her alone. He kept saying he knew the best way to cheer her up and telling her she should come back to his place. In the end I had to say something. I went over and told them all to leave her alone. I was shitting myself to be honest. I've never been in a fight in my life and they looked pretty rough. The big one squared up to me but the bloke behind the counter threatened to call the police so they all left." Chris finally takes a breath from machine-gunning the words at me.

"Fucking hell Chris," I say, genuinely impressed. "You could have got a right kicking there." I have to hand it to him. It's one thing having a ruck when you love a bit of a scuffle like me and the lads, but sticking your neck out when you've never thrown a punch in your life. That's proper brave. He could have got a right pasting. I can't hide my admiration. I wonder if I would have done the same thing.

Turns out he sat with her for a while to calm her down. He even managed to cheer her up a bit. She forgot about the group of lads and whatever it was she was crying about. Then he walked her home. A full forty-five minutes in the opposite direction to where he was going. Christ, you wouldn't catch me doing something like that. Put her in a cab maybe, but walking all that way, no chance.

He's bouncing around like a puppy as he tells me they're going out sometime next week. Fair play to him. He must be odds on for a shag. Maybe being decent pays off every now and again. I wonder if it's an angle I should try sometime. I could do with a change in luck. I think that ship may have sailed for me with Amy, though unfortunately. The look on her face last night pops into my head again and the embarrassment creeps back across my face. I push it away. Maybe if I don't picture it then it didn't really happen.

The truth is I'm gutted about the whole stupid episode. I head back into my room and try to call her. She doesn't answer. I didn't think she would to be fair. I text her. Tell her how sorry I am. That I didn't mean to behave like that last night and that I hope she can forgive me. She doesn't reply. She probably just needs some time to think about it all.

The fact I only got up at four o'clock doesn't seem to make any difference and by nine I'm desperate to crawl back into my bed. The stench of stale alcohol still clouds the air, so I open up the windows and climb under the covers. I leave my phone next to me on the pillow, with vibrate on and the ringtone volume turned up, just in case Amy gets back to me while I'm asleep.

She doesn't.

Chapter Twenty-five

I've got a bit of bruising around the jaw on Monday morning but the swelling's gone down a bit. David gives me a look but doesn't say anything. Charlie comes over to see if I'm alright. I give him the short version over in the kitchenette while we're making the teas. I think he feels a bit bad that he wasn't there to help out. He used to love a good tear up back in the day. He suggests going for a catch up at lunchtime, which'll be decent. It feels like a few weeks since we've had a proper laugh together.

He's got some paperwork to sort out this morning from the flat he sold at the end of last week. I need to get one of these houses flogged or I'll have no chance of catching him. Nick's on the phone just after nine-thirty, wanting a progress report on Mrs O'Shea's. I tell him I'll give her solicitor a bell straight away.

"Danny, can I have a word?" asks David, as soon as I'm off the phone. We go and sit at his desk. It's a bit more private. He likes to call it his office, but really it's just a slightly larger desk at the back of the room.

"What's up David?" I say. I don't feel like playing the Dave card and winding him up this morning. I haven't got the energy for it. I'm still a bit flat from the weekend and possibly still a touch hungover.

"We've had a bit of a complaint about you I'm afraid," he says, lowering his voice. This is all I need this morning. Alice is sitting about four feet away and pretending she's not listening in but the dumb mare is incapable of doing two things at once so the fact she's immediately stopped typing is a bit of a giveaway.

"Oh really?" I ask. "Who from?"

"A young couple named Marcus and Jo-Jo. I believe you showed them around Mrs Baker's property on Friday. The young lady called this morning to say you were extremely rude to them. Is this true?"

Fucking Marcus and Jo-Jo. "I wouldn't say I was rude to them David, I just pointed out that they couldn't possibly afford the house they were insisting on viewing. They're a pair of timewasters. We had loads of proper buyers viewing it as well, so what's the problem?"

"That's as maybe Danny, but the brand comes first. Barrie and Aberdeen, cannot afford our good name to be tarnished, especially with all this social media nonsense these days. I've decided the best course of action is to bring them in so that you can apologise to them for your conduct face to face."

David must have finally lost his marbles. "Are you shitting me?" I say, trying very hard to keep a lid on my rage. "I'm not going to apologise to them David, absolutely no chance. Not even if my job depends on it."

"Well," he says, all flustered. He can't afford to lose his top sales guy, certainly not over this total bullshit. "I've already told them you'd do it. They're coming in at three this afternoon."

"Then you'd better do it Dave, there's not a hope in hell of me apologising that pair of numpties." I storm straight out of the office. I'm aware I may be overplaying my hand here, but I'm seeing red. I fly past Alice, who pretends not to have heard anything by staring at her computer screen as if it's the first one she's ever seen.

I head straight to The Bison and Bird and order a pint. I text Charlie to say I've gone for an early lunch and I'll wait for him in the pub. I start to simmer down a bit as the beer hits my system. I suppose it's not David's fault really, he has to act on these things, but there is no way I'm apologising to those dickheads. What the fuck is wrong with everyone these days. You can't tell it like it is anymore. Everyone's too desperate to take offence at every little thing.

I pass the time waiting for Charlie by going through my dating options. Ellie's off, although she's keen on meeting up this week for a final session. One last night for the road before she ups sticks to Australia to ride Kangaroos and shag blokes with tribal tattoos. I've got nothing else planned so I may as well. We'll probably do Thursday night. For old time's sake.

Looks like Amy's out the picture too. She still hasn't replied to my last message. I try to recall the last time she replied to anything. I can't. And that was before I tried to thump her new bloke. Sophie didn't take kindly to being binned off, so I can cross her off the list. Michelle's still floating about but the thought doesn't excite me too much. She's got a great body but truly shite chat. I realise the cupboard's looking pretty bare, so I get on Tinder.

I swipe right to a couple, get a couple of quick matches. I realise one of them's got that Marilyn Monroe quote as one of her pictures. *"If you can't handle me at my worst, then you sure as hell don't deserve me at my best."* I delete and block her immediately. I send a message to an absolute cracker called Hannah. She's got definite potential. I half-heartedly chat to someone called Donna. She's a little older than I would normally consider, at thirty-seven, but she looks alright in her pictures. A good back up option.

Charlie comes in and offers me a drink before he heads to the bar. I'm halfway through my pint so I ask him for another. He comes back with my Stella. He's on the diet cokes. I call him gay but he ignores my bants and cuts straight to the chase. He wants to know about the weekend. I start telling him all about the big win at the pub before he interrupts me. "I meant the fight."

I knew he'd be spoiling for the details. He was a decent boxer in his teenage years by all accounts. Always been handy if it ever kicks off on a night out. I give him all the details. I've got over it a bit now, so I can see the funny side of it. I reckon you've got to laugh at yourself sometimes.

He interrupts me again. "Mate, I don't think it's very funny."

"Christ," I say, "someone's had a banter bypass. What's been up with you these last few weeks?"

He sighs. "Look, I've been meaning to have a word with you for a while now. Is this really what you want to keep doing? Still going out like you're eighteen, shagging different birds every night and getting into fights? Don't you want anything more out of life?"

I look at him like he has finally lost his fucking mind.

"Don't get all defensive mate," he says, pre-empting the outburst he knows is coming, "I'm just trying to look out for you."

Look out for me? If he wanted to look out for me, he should have been there when some jumped up little prick was having a swing at me.

"Fuck off Charlie." I say. "What the fuck's happened to you mate. You've gone soft. Never out with the lads anymore. Going home early when you do come out. Sucking up to David at work. Just fuck off and leave me to my pint."

He stands up and looks like he wants to say something. I stare at my beer and refuse to make eye contact. He walks away. For fuck's sake. I'll have no one left at this rate. I take my time with my pint, order a steak sandwich, and have a think about what to do. I call David.

"Hi David," I say, before he has a chance to get stuck into me. "I'm sorry about earlier, but I was very upset about the accusation they've made. Especially as I've had a bit of a bad weekend." It's important to go for the sympathy angle early in these situations. "I totally agree with you about the brand name being important," I bullshit, "but what with my bruised face and these headaches I've been getting all morning, I think it might be best if you can pass on my apologies to the couple on my behalf. If it's ok with you, I might go the doctor's and get checked out. Ever since I got this bang on the jaw I've been getting these terrible migraines."

He thinks for a while, before reluctantly agreeing to my plan. He suggests I get myself straight to the doctor's surgery. I can tell from his tone he doesn't really believe me. But what can he do? He'd be well in the shit if it turned out to be true and I keeled over in the office.

I put down the phone. Now I've got the afternoon off I order myself another pint.

Chapter Twenty-six

Despite having a semi-hangover from the five pints I got through at the pub on Monday afternoon, Tuesday feels like a different day altogether. I get two offers in for Mrs Baker's house. The first from the young couple. They offer four-eighty, which is not a bad start at all considering it's on at five-hundred.

I'm just about to call to tell her about the offer when Mr Business-like calls and offers four-seven-five, which puts me in a bit of a dilemma. The young couple's offer is better and technically, *technically*, I'm supposed to put every offer forward, but the lower offer is hassle free, and will complete much quicker. Unfortunately for the young couple I need the sale quickly if I'm going to have a hope of catching Charlie and getting that bonus, so I call Mrs Baker and give her the good news. Well, some of it anyway.

"Great news Mrs Baker," I say as she picks up the phone, "We've had a great offer from one of Friday's viewings. Four-Seven-Five. No chain. They want to move quickly."

"That's fantastic," she says. She's doing the maths in her head, I can practically hear the cogs turning. "Is anyone else interested or is this the best offer we're going to get?"

"It's the only offer we've had so far," I lie, "and I definitely think it's worth strongly considering. Do you want to have a think about it and get back to me?" She agrees to give me a call later to let me know her thoughts. I put the phone down and look over at the leaderboard. Charlie's managed to get himself six-hundred grand in front, but if I can push this through I'll be right on his tail with a few weeks to go. With the O'Shea sale already with the solicitors I'm in with a good shout. There's no way Mrs Baker won't take the offer. I'll make sure of it.

I finally get a Tinder reply off that Hannah chick and we have a brief chat. Turns out she works in finance or something up in town. Fancy. I don't tell her I'm an estate agent as for some reason it puts some people off. I'm probably a bit different to the high-flyers she's used to up in central, but once I've given her a bit of chat, and hopefully a bit of a seeing to, she'll forget all about that. She's busy most of the week but we arrange to meet up on Sunday afternoon for a couple of drinks. I try to get some banter going, but its hard work. I give her my number in case she wants to chat away from Tinder. Moving communication away from the dating site as soon as possible is one of my big strategies. It makes the situation seem more organic. More *normal*. I don't get a reply straight back. She's probably really busy at work.

Things with Charlie thaw out a bit when he comes over to my desk to break the ice in the afternoon. He apologises for everything he said yesterday. I tell him I don't mind. Forget about it, I say, despite the fact it's the one thing I can't do. *Forget about it*. What he said yesterday's been rattling around my head ever since. I was angry to start with but the more it's sunk in the more the thought occurred to me that maybe he's onto something. Maybe if I hadn't fucked it up with Amy so badly I wouldn't be scrabbling around desperately searching for new girls to fill my rapidly emptying social calendar.

I'll be a bit more careful in the future. Keep the number of girls down to two or three at a time. I need to make things more manageable. Maybe only go out a couple of times a week. I don't tell him any of this. I don't want him to think I'm giving him permission to get back on his high horse and give me another lecture. He suggests going for lunch on Friday. It'll be good to get back in the old routine.

Mrs Baker calls back later on, wanting me to go over to discuss the offer. The young couple call again wanting an update. I inform them that unfortunately we've had a higher offer. They're gutted. The four-eighty was the absolute maximum they could stretch to and they had their hearts set on it. I tell them I'll see if we've got anything else on the books that might be suitable. With a bit of luck I'll be able to push them onto something else and end up with another sale. It's that kind of brain power that sets me apart from other estate agents.

I get round to Mrs Baker's in the afternoon. She's covered up a bit more this time. There's still a hell of a cleavage on show, but the rest of her top half is safely tucked away underneath a black vest top. "So what do you think I should do?" she asks as we both lean against opposite worktops in the family kitchen. I try not to stare at her tits too much. The remnants of the half-eaten sandwich she had for lunch sit on a plate next to the sink. Ham and cheese by the look of it.

All the anger and the furious energy seem to have ebbed away slightly since the last time I saw her. The fire in her eyes has gone. She looks tired and sad. Like all the rage has been peeled away. Now all that's left is the magnitude of what lies ahead. She looks like she just wants to be put out of her misery. I tell her she should take the offer. They're keen and want to move quickly. She can draw a line under the whole thing and start to move on once she and the kids are taken care of and living somewhere else. Somewhere not haunted by the memories of how things used to be.

She tries to put on a bit of front. Mentions something about inviting me round for a celebratory drink when it all goes through, but her heart's not in it. I can see it in her eyes. I tell her I'll be in touch and head back to the office to let the buyer know it's a yes. I hope to Christ I don't end up like that.

I go straight back to David when I'm back and ask him for a quick word in his office. I apologise for the day before. It feels like the right thing to do. It doesn't strike me as a good career move, being at odds with the boss, even if he is a total bell-end. I promise him it won't happen again, blame it on the difficult time I've been going through over the last few weeks. He seems pleased I've come to my senses. He's never been one to enjoy conflict, so I think he's just glad the situation is defused. I tell him the good news about Mrs. Baker's place. That tips things back over the edge and I'm back in the good books.

I head back to my desk to tell the buyer their offer's been accepted. I pass the leaderboard on my way and give it a tap to tell Charlie he's not got it in the bag just yet. He grins at me and if feels like maybe everything's getting back on track. I leave a message for Mrs O'Shea's solicitor to see where we are with her sale. I need to keep this momentum going.

I get home and Chris is standing there in the hallway, all ready for his big date. He's got a checked shirt on, a new pair of jeans and his best pair of shoes. He looks decent. He's still going strong with the new diet and the running and it's taken half a stone off him by the looks of it. Amazing how fast it falls off when you stop chucking pizza down your throat. They're going down to The Windmill for a few drinks and a bit of food. It's his first date since his ex fucked him off. He is absolutely shitting himself.

I wish him good luck and I'm surprised to realise I mean it. The blokes had a shitty few months and deserves a bit of good luck. I give him a fist-bump before he disappears out into the early evening half-light. I head to the living room to see if he's got any movies that aren't about dinosaurs or spaceships and end up picking up some weird thing called Game of Thrones that he's been banging on about for ages.

Chapter Twenty-seven

Ellie's lying on my bed, scrolling through her Instagram feed, checking the number of followers she's got compared to other female personal trainers. She seems happy enough with the results, although still needs to get my opinion on whether her arse is better than some of the other girls she comes across a few times. She even stands up and bends over at one point so that I can compare the images on her phone to her own cheeks which are squeezed into a tiny leopard-print thong millimetres from my face. She doesn't understand why it so funny.

I'm next to her, absent-mindedly watching the TV, which I finally managed to fix back to the wall yesterday afternoon. I left if for a couple of days but trying to watch the Chelsea's Champions League match last night on a wonky TV was bloody murder. Chris gave me a hand, which made things easier. There's no way I would have been able to do it myself. He's out with that Ruby chick again tonight, their second date in three days. They must both be keen as mustard.

He was absolutely buzzing when he got back from the first one on Tuesday night. He burst through the door when I was just getting into that Game of Thrones thing. Didn't think it'd be my thing to be honest, what with all that medieval bollocks and bloody dragons. Turns out I was wrong. Lots more tits than I expected. And an absolute sort of a blonde bird in it as well. Chris came back in from his date right when she was getting a right seeing to from some beardy caveman.

Chris barely noticed, just started babbling about his date with Ruby. About how pretty she is. How brown her eyes are. How much she makes him laugh. Bouncing around the room he was. I listened while I kept my eye on the blonde. She didn't seem to be enjoying the caveman's technique. It has to be said it was a little on the rough side. Chris let slip he walked Ruby home again. Another forty-odd minute stroll at the end of the night. Didn't get a kiss from her though. I had to pull him up on that. The gentleman angle is all well and good but there's only so long you can play it. All girls get bored if all you ever do is open doors and hold their chairs out for them. There's a happy medium somewhere between Chris and this caveman geezer, and in my experience it's a lot closer to the caveman. Still, things must be looking up for him as I haven't heard a note of that awful music of his recently.

Ellie closes her Instagram and starts showing me pictures of where she's going in Australia. It's all waterfalls and big rocks and turquoise water. Looks decent to be fair. I can see why people want to go all the way over there. It's all open space and colour. Over here everything just shades of grey. The only lights shining through the shit are the signs from Starbucks, McDonald's and Paddy Power. Not much of a comparison now I think about it.

She keeps dropping hints about me going over there to meet up with her. She reckons it'd broaden my horizons to see new places and meet different kinds of people. She reminds me of my girlfriend back in Bournemouth when she talks like that. She was always talking about seeing the world and going on adventures. She dumped me the day after graduation and did all that with someone else instead. I stopped thinking about all that kind of stuff after that. The biggest trip I've ever done was to Vegas with the lads a couple of years ago. Brilliant it was. Non-stop gambling, boozing and strippers. The clubs out there are on a different planet. Maybe when I get my next bonus from Nick I'll have a think about going somewhere new, see a bit more of the world.

The two hours we've spent next to each other on the bed chatting and looking at pictures is the longest time we've spent together with our clothes on since the first time we met. I take her phone out of her hand and put a stop to that, but the reckless abandon we're both used to isn't there. It's measured and quiet, almost intimate. Like we both know it's the final time, and we want to make sure we make it last. Ironic really, the only time Chris isn't in is the only time he doesn't need his earplugs.

We both lie there in sweaty silence for a few minutes afterwards. It's not awkward though. We're both content, there's no need to say anything. She's back to thinking of Australia I'm sure. I'm trying not to think about anything in particular.

"Do you want to watch Donnie Brasco?" I ask. "Actually watch it I mean."

She laughs. "Yeah, stick it on, it'd be nice to know what actually happens."

We lie there for the next few hours, watching the film unfold, Ellie propped up on my shoulder, my arm round her. We watch Al Pacino walk off to his death at the end and she's rubbing her eyes, trying to pretend she's not crying. She's half asleep on me when I hear Chris come back through the front door. He's whistling. Sounds like the date went well. Can't have gone that well though as he's home on his own.

Ellie takes her time getting ready in the morning, walking around completely naked for a good fifteen minutes. I can't tell if she's doing it because she doesn't want to leave, or if it's because she wants to burn the image of her body into my memory. As if that's necessary. I've got countless photos and videos of her on my phone. She barely goes a few days without sending one. She finally puts on her gym gear for her last shift at work. She gives me a hug that turns into a cuddle. It lasts a couple of silent minutes. "I'll send you some pictures from over there," she says with a wink. She turns to look at me one last time and she's rubbing her eyes again. I think we both know this will be the last time we see each other.

I try to work out how I feel while I stand under a scalding shower for the next ten minutes. There's that same feeling I felt when I visited Mrs Baker's place the first time. When I walked around inside a half-empty house. Through dust and boxes and silence. I could tell someone used to be there, that they'd been erased as best they could, but you could still see the space they used to occupy. That's how I feel as I let the water pound against my face. That something's missing. Like there's a gap inside somewhere that no-one's filled up. My relationship with Ellie was purely sexual, we didn't even have much in common outside the bedroom, but it's impossible not to feel a bit empty when someone who's been around for a long time says goodbye. Or maybe it just reminded me of everybody else who's said goodbye over the years. I drag myself out of the shower and head into the office. There's a message from Mrs O'Shea's solicitor to call him back. I think about the old dear, on her own in another empty house. Surrounding by empty spaces that used to be filled up. I push it away. Being a soft fucker doesn't make you any money in this game. I call him back. Everything's on schedule. The sale should go through in the next couple of weeks. Just in time for the end of the year. I message Hannah. Hopefully we're still on for our date on Sunday. I don't want to end up on my own like all these other fuckers.

Chapter Twenty-eight

Charlie mentions the leaderboard Friday lunchtime. He can't help it, he thinks he's got it all sewn up. I can't resist wiping the smug grin off his face. I tell him how close the Mrs O'Shea sale is to going through. That does the trick. He's doing the maths in his head and realises I'm going to pip him to the post. "I still don't understand why she took such a low offer," he says. "That place was worth eight-hundred at least." Charlie can be so dense sometimes. As we're a couple of pints in and back to being friends again I decide to let him in on the secret. I tell him about the deal I've got with Nick.

"So that's how you've got the flat and that flashy motor?" he says. The penny finally drops. I offer to put them in touch as sort of an olive branch after the recent argument we had. He's interested. I tell him all about the solicitor who gives me a kickback and my mate who does the surveys.

"Isn't that fraud?" he says.

"How's anyone ever going to find out?" I answer. He nods. He gets it. I give him Nick's number, tell him I'll set up a meeting. Charlie gets the next round in to say thanks. It's the least he can do to be fair. Me putting him in touch with Nick could be worth a few grand a year in his pocket.

"So you been dating much the last few weeks?" he asks when he's back from the bar with the drinks.

"Not really." I say. He looks surprised. I tell him I never heard back from Amy after my attempt to apologise. I tell him I've seen the last of Ellie as well now. I tell him about Sunday's date with Hannah. "After what you said the other day, and seeing Chris getting a bird, I was thinking I should give this whole *nice guy* angle a go. At least see how it goes with this Hannah bird anyway."

"It's not an angle mate," he says.

I laugh at him. Yeah right. He must think I was born yesterday. "What about you though mate?" I ask, "Gaz reckons you've got a bird."

"There is one girl I've been seeing a bit of," he says. He's never been one to give too much away. "I'm meeting a couple of her mates tomorrow night actually, so I won't be out with the lads again."

"Bloody hell," I say, "meeting the mates. Must be serious. At this rate you'll be pulling out of coming to Marbs." He laughs and takes another sip of his pint to avoid answering the question.

"I'm going to give Saturday a miss as well to be honest." I say to him on the way back to the office." I want to make sure I'm not hanging out of my arse for my date with this Hannah chick." He looks impressed. Like a dad who's proud of how far his son's come. He can be a right patronising prick sometimes.

I spend the rest of the afternoon waiting for the clock to hit five. Literally nothing happens. No viewings, no phone calls, nothing. I order the second season of Game of Thrones to make sure it arrives on Monday. I'll have finished the first by the end of the weekend if I'm staying in on Saturday night. Chris gets back to the flat about seven. The prick's actually run home from the office. Must be at least eight miles. He'll be training for the marathon at this rate. His face isn't even that red anymore when he gets back. He reckons he's lost a stone over the last three weeks. You can see it as well.

"Fancy a pizza tonight?" I ask. It's like I've offered an alcoholic a bottle of vodka. Pain, fear, lust and hunger all cycle through the expression on his face.

He stays strong though. "Better not," he says, "Ruby's coming over tomorrow for takeaway and a movie."

"Last night must have gone well then?" I say. He moves straight into the gushing phase and begins taking me through a blow by blow account of the entire date. I'm happy for him and everything but I'm buggered if I'm going to listen to him drone on for the next hour about the texture of the king prawn linguine he had at Zizzi's. I interrupt and cut to the chase. "Did you get any?"

His face returns to the familiar tomato-coloured hue from that first run a few weeks ago. "We may have had a little kiss at the end of the evening," he confirms, after a fair bit of stammering.

"A kiss?" I say. "Is that it? What is this? A fucking Disney film."

He clams up a bit, almost sulking as he mumbles, "We aren't all sex maniacs you know."

Fucking hell, I was only teasing. He never was much good with the banter. "I'm only joking mate, I'm happy for you, I really am." I realise that I actually am.

Hannah finally replies to me just after nine. I can't lie, I was starting to get a bit antsy. She apologises, says she's been snowed under at work. She's looking forward to Sunday.

Gaz is in a right mood at the gym Saturday morning when I tell him that I'm not out with the lads later on. He reckons they've got no chance of pulling any birds if it's just him and Ritz. Ben's away on some dodgy trip to Estonia. I shudder to think what he's up to. I don't say anything but Gaz is probably right. In the end I just tell him to make sure he gets his arms out and the girl's will be queuing up. It doesn't convince him though and he heads off home in a sulk, without the traditional warm down in the sauna and Jacuzzi. I meet the pair of them in the pub for Soccer Saturday but they're both in a mood by that point. Evidently Gaz has mentioned it's just those two out tonight. I stay until half time but the boys barely say a word. All our bets are fucked by this point anyway, so I tell them I'm heading off home. They grunt in my direction by way of saying goodbye. They can be a right pair of mongs those two.

Chris comes in with Ruby halfway through my Game of Thrones marathon, right in the middle of a brothel scene, which is a bit embarrassing. As first impressions go, assuming someone is spending their Saturday evening watching medieval porn is probably not the best. I pause it when they both come in, unfortunately right in the middle of a scene with at least three visible pairs of tits. Ruby's cool though. She laughs. She seems nice. Quiet. A bit shy even. Although maybe that's down to the tits frozen all over the TV screen.

She's pretty. Really pretty actually. Chris is batting well above his average again. I don't know how he does it. Must be this whole Mr Nice Guy angle he's got going on. They go off to get their takeaway from down the road while I watch the last episode of season one. Sean Bean gets his head chopped off. Mental. I thought he was the star of the whole programme. I spent the whole episode assuming he'd get out of it, even when some massive bloke was standing over him with a fucking great sword. Then his head's off and the credits role. I nearly spat out my Domino's.

Chris and Ruby come back with a Nando's and cuddle up on the sofa like a proper little couple. We watch some sugary rom-com with Ryan Gosling. It's a welcome relief after old Sean came a cropper. I head off to bed about eleven leaving the lovebirds to it on the sofa.

I'm standing outside Richmond station waiting for Hannah and I start to panic. It's always a risk speaking to a stonking bird on a dating site. Her pictures might be great but you don't know how old they are. She might have turned into a right heifer since the pictures were taken. You can never be too sure. I found that out a couple of years ago. The bird turned up about four stone heavier than her pictures, with a completely different hair colour. It turned out her pictures were seven years old.

I needn't have worried on this occasion. Hannah's a firecracker, I can see that from a few hundred metres away as she strolls down the road towards me. She kisses me on the cheek as she says hello and her scent tingles over my senses. She smells fucking delicious. She looks amazing, even for just a simple afternoon in the pub. She's a half foot shorter than me and somehow makes the simple jeans and top combo look like a catwalk outfit. She's got this slightly tanned complexion and light brown hair. Big lips. Almost a European feel to her. She's a proper sort. I mentally high-five myself as we head down to a couple of the pubs I've singled out as options. We're in Richmond, well outside my normal patch but I've done my research. There's a couple of pubs I've picked out with great views across the hills down to the river that snakes off into the distance. If there's one thing I know how to do, it's sort out a decent location for a date.

I head to the bar and grab us some drinks. I steal a glance back at her while I'm waiting for the greasy muppet behind the bar. She's fucking fit and no mistake. I sit back and let her do most of the talking. Girls love a listener. It really marks you out as different apparently. It's easy to sit and watch a girl talking though when she looks like Hannah. It's only the real troglodytes with zero banter you have to drive the conversation with. It turns out she's half-French, which explains the European thing she's got going on. Top drawer.

What starts with a couple of drinks in the afternoon stretches well into a Sunday night dinner date. The first moment of awkwardness arrives with the bill. I make the move to pay, but Hannah asks to do the honours. I'm not keen. I reckon if I'm going to play the nice guy card then it's important I pay, especially on the first date. I insist. Hannah insists right back again. I think maybe she's one of those girl power types, like Geri Spice or something, so I relent and agree to go halves, before it gets really awkward. I use it to my advantage though, as a ruse for getting another date. I agree to the fifty-fifty as long as she lets me take her out for dinner the following week. She agrees. Awkwardness averted and the go ahead for date number two achieved. Result.

We make our way slowly back to the tube station, a full six and a half hours after we met. We're both pretty pissed by this point, and the sun's long since faded across the fields below us, replaced by a pale moon that's piercing through the night cover of clouds. We're not really in the vicinity of my flat or hers, which is something I overlooked when selecting the venue, which pretty much rules out a shag. I suppose a nice guy wouldn't try that on a first date actually, so maybe it's not a bad thing.

We stop to say goodbye at the entrance. She stands on tip-toes and full-on kisses me, no hesitation, no holding back. She surprises me with her urgency. If I'm not mistaken she's got the horn. I start to regret playing the nice guy card. She walks through the barriers and disappears.

I stand at the station for a minute or so to catch my breath. And to let my boner go down. I curse my decision to not organise the date at a venue nearer home. I scan her pictures on Facebook in the cab home. We aren't friends but I can see enough to know she's got a great body on her. She's a good laugh as well, a definite contender for my vacant Friday night slot. She messages me as I'm walking through the front door, thanking me for a lovely night. She's definitely keen.

Chapter Twenty-nine

Mr Business-Like really comes through on the sale of the Baker house. His solicitor calls Wednesday morning to let me know they're due to exchange contracts on Friday, and complete the following week. His wife must have really wanted the place. It'll be barely three weeks end to end by the time it's gone through. I tell the solicitor to make sure the cash he owes me is in my bank account before the exchange goes through. I don't want him weaselling out of my referral fee.

I call Mrs Baker to check she's in the loop. She sounds really down. The cold realisation that she and the kids will be living with her parents until she finds somewhere else must have hit her by now. She'll be packing up what's left of her life into cardboard boxes for the next few days. Then they'll be crammed into her parents' place and someone else will be all moved in within two weeks. It'll be like they never lived there.

Her tone is dead and she's lost all her energy. She sounds exhausted. She doesn't even bother flirting. It's the kids I feel sorry for. Their lives turned upside down because their dad couldn't keep his knob under control. No more family meals around the table, no more holidays away. Just sleeping top and tail in their grandparents' house while their mum tries to hold their lives together.

Charlie and I go for lunch with Nick in the same clandestine old pub he always insists on meeting in. David's out all day at a monthly sales update with the big bosses so we've got plenty of time. We're already sitting in an alcove at the back when Nick arrives and announces himself with a cheery 'alwight lads' and a quick handshake. I'm not sure why, but he always puts on a fake cockney accent when he's trying to impress people. Like he's some kind of dodgy wheeler-dealer. It does him a disservice. He doesn't need to pretend anything to anyone. The bloke's got millions in the bank.

I introduce him to Charlie and his tone changes. He looks me dead in the eyes, even moves his Miami vice sunglasses up onto his forehead as he asks, "can we trust him?" Meaning Charlie, who just sits there awkwardly, until I reply.

"Course we can," I say to Nick, "he's my best mate."

"Well that's alwight then," he says in his daft accent. He's all smiles again as he lays out the deal to Charlie. How it works, how important it is that we get the properties to him before they go on the market. He gives his speech about time-pressure and runs through the types of people who are likely to sell under market value; Divorcees, recent widowers, probate lawyers with families looking to get their hands on some quick inheritance cash.

"People in lots of debt?" asks Charlie.

"This one catches on quick," says Nick, impressed. As if I would have put any old numpty in front of him. He orders us some lunch and pays on his black Amex card, while he runs through some of the best deals he's ever done. I've heard the spiel before but it's impossible not to be impressed. Millions and millions in property and he's hardly used a penny of his own cash. It's all about leverage with Nick. He bangs on about *OPM*. Other People's Money. By that he means banks. Mortgages. Business loans. Bridging loans. Loads of stuff I never knew existed before I met Nick.

We shake hands in the car park afterwards and watch him speed off in his Range Rover Sport until it's out of sight. Charlie's practically got a lob on.

Charlie's got the rest of the afternoon off so I've been lumbered with some viewing he's got booked in on a dingy studio flat in the arse-end of Stockwell. It's been on the books for over a year now. I'm pretty sure the owners have given up on ever getting shot of it.

Some bloke turns up to see it. He looks a right state. Crumpled suit, a straggly beard scrawled all over his face. His tie's hanging off his neck as if he's come straight from being bullied in the school playground. I show him the flat, which takes about four seconds. There's a hybrid kitchen- bedroom- living room-diner room, which is about fifteen feet square. The only other room is a walk-in bathroom, about the size of the shitter back at the office, and in marginally worse condition. There's a shower and toilet inside. It's been turned into a wet room, purely for the space efficiency. The place is rank. It's an absolute hole and no mistake. Unfortunately for this sad-act it's the only thing within his tiny budget.

"As you can see," I say, gesturing to the tatty carpet and peeling wallpaper, "it's a real fixer-upper."

He looks at me with the dead eyes of someone who's well beyond caring about décor. "How much is it on for?" he asks.

"One-thirty."

"I can do one-twenty," he says, with absolutely zero enthusiasm.

"I'll put that forward to the vendor, and get their thoughts on it," I say. Christ, they won't believe their luck. "What's your current situation?" I ask, "so that I can present your offer in the best light."

"I'm getting divorced," he says, "the wife's selling the house at the moment, but she'll keep most of the money. Only fair, as she's got the kids with her. There's not much left over once she takes what she needs so this will have to do me. I've been in a B&B down the road for the last month, so the sooner we can tie this up the better as far as I'm concerned." He looks around the flat once more time like a prisoner being shown to his cell; ready to start a life sentence.

"I'm pretty confident they'll take the offer," I say, trying to shine a fraction of positive light onto his predicament, as we head back down the car park behind the block of flats. A feral kid throws a stone at a burnt-out car in the corner. The gang of youngsters huddled around it look us over with interest. One of them shouts "Oi wankers," at us. They can't be older than fourteen. At least three of them are smoking and one's got a can of Strongbow. The bloke shrugs and gets into his car. He doesn't really look like he cares about anything anymore.

I give Charlie a call to let him know the news. "You owe me a beer," I say, "I've just managed to get shot of Shire Court to that loser you booked in for a viewing."

He's totally unsurprised, which pisses on my parade a bit. "Yeah, I thought he'd probably take it," he says. "His wife kicked him out. Caught him with the au pair apparently. The bloke's got nowhere else to go. He's completely fucked."

The look in Mr Baker's eyes when I showed him round that shithole haunts me for the rest of the day. It's only me and Colin in the office, so I tell him I've got a dentist appointment in case he grasses me up, and nip off early. I get myself a four-pack of Stellas on the way back.

I sink the first can in a couple of gulps. I can see his face again. The look in his eyes. Of defeat. His life ruined, living in a stinking shithole of a room. His wife and kids living with her parents, turfed out of their family home so they can sell up and go their separate ways. All because he couldn't keep his dick in his pants. That au pair must have been seriously fit. Is that where I'm heading? Fuck that. I'm not ending up like that dishevelled, beaten-down loser, stuck on his own, too old to start over, a life time of punishing himself for his mistakes ahead of him. I drop Hannah a message mid-way through the third beer. It's been a couple of days since we last spoke. I need to get that second date in the diary before she thinks I'm not interested. I'm not ending up like that loser.

Chapter Thirty

The exchange goes through on Mrs Baker's house with no hitches. I mark it down on the leaderboard. It's a bit early, as it doesn't complete until the end of next week, but I want Charlie to see me snapping at his heels. I let him take the glory of shifting that shithole studio flat to Mr Baker, even though I was the one who got it over the line and made the sale. It makes me look generous, and the measly hundred and twenty grand isn't going to make any difference once Mrs O'Shea's house goes through. That bonus is going in my pocket. I can almost imagine the cash I'll have to spend in Marbella.

David shakes my hand and tells me how happy he is with my recent performance at work, the dickhead. Hannah finally replies to me about sorting out our dinner date. It's been two days, but again, she apologises profusely. It's month end at work apparently, which in the finance world means you have to work all hours of the day and night. Sounds pretty shit to me. She can only do Tuesday next week for dinner. Not exactly my first choice but I take it. I need to get some momentum going. If Tuesday goes well maybe I can lock something in for the weekend, start to try to close the deal. Maybe even offer to make her dinner on Saturday night. That'd be a definite shag.

She's a bit standoffish over text. I need to break her down with a bit of my textbook banter so I send her a couple of messages back. She doesn't reply. This month end stuff must be a nightmare, the poor girl barely has time for a conversation. I spend the afternoon doing a bit of research online to find a nice restaurant up in town. Something expensive. I get the impression Hannah is the sort of bird I need to impress. Show her I mean business. She's classier than the birds I normally put away. Not the sort you'd find on Inferno's dancefloor at two in the morning.

I feel like I need to get right into character with this nice guy angle. Properly immerse myself in it. It's shit timing as Chris and Ruby are down in Brighton shagging their brains out and traditionally I'd take advantage of the empty flat by boning someone. There's no Amy or Ellie but I've still got a few options. Michelle's still on the case, wanting another round with the champ, obviously. That Donna off Tinder would be easy to get round as well, even though we haven't met yet. She's been bombarding me with messages since I first matched with her, wanting to go out. It's doing my head in a bit. She's only a backup for fuck's sake, she needs to wind her neck in.

In the end I use the nice guy routine as a get out clause. Tell her I'm seeing someone now, that I don't want to be one of those guys that dates multiple women. I don't even laugh when I'm writing it. It's amazing how easy it is to get on your high horse about something once you really start to believe it. The stupid thing is it makes her even more up for it, but I do the decent thing and resist. Besides, Donna doesn't strike me as the most stable tree in the orchard.

I head over to Nando's for the standard Friday night takeaway. Pieter says hello. He recognises me now. It's taken him long enough. I see a bit of pity in his eyes sometimes, like I'm some poor dumped loser ordering a Nando's for one. I want to tell him that I was the one who didn't want to be tied down, not Amy, so technically, *technically*, I chucked her, but I reckon that might make me look a bit mental, so I leave it. He remembers the Perinaise though, which is a fucking miracle.

I get back to the flat and chug through the cans of Stella I picked up at the corner shop on the way home. I get through them and halfway into the bottle of Pinot while I watch another couple of episodes of Game of Thrones. I think about Mr Baker again as I sink into my boozy cloud. I wonder what he's doing. Probably something not a million miles from this. Maybe he's got the au pair with him. He may as well have, there's no coming back for him now. I can still see his hollow eyes when I close mine and doze off on the sofa.

It's been a couple of weeks since we've had a proper session so I meet the lads down at the pub for Soccer Saturday. Even Charlie comes down for the first time in weeks. Ben sticks a bet on Wayne Rooney to score first for Man United which comes in. A hundred quid in his skyrocket. Gaz and Ritz want to do Inferno's later but me and Charlie aren't keen. He's got an early start in the morning and I've got one eye on the Hannah situation. I don't want to go out and get shitfaced and end up doinking some bird while I'm trying this nice guy stuff out, so we just stay at the pub and get leathered. Proper battered like the old days. Banter. Shot. Pint. Banter. Shot. Pint. Fucking great night. Ritz has got some gear on him again, but I only do a couple of lines. If I go too far down that road I'll end up roaming Inferno's until three in the morning.

Charlie doesn't touch it at all, says he's given up the stuff. He drink a lot less than us as well, only gets half-cut to our smashed. There's a lot of talk about the summer lads' trip. Even Charlie seems keen. I tell them if I get this bonus I'll stump up half the cash for a villa in Marbella, which goes down a storm. The end of the night comes with our traditional serenade of John in the kebab shop. His name's not John of course, I think it's something like Mohammed or Ahmed. He likes us calling him John though. Makes him feel like one of the lads. Loves the banter that bloke.

I get home just after midnight. Michelle messages, asking what I'm up to. A blatant booty call. I'm sorely tempted but I don't reply. I need to stay strong, keep going with the nice guy angle. I've heard nothing from Hannah since Friday lunchtime. She's obviously not a big texter. The flat's quiet without Chris and Ruby. Being home alone at this time on a Saturday night isn't a regular scenario so I'm not really sure what to do with myself. I have a look through Ellie's Instagram. Various pictures of her getting off the plane in Perth. A couple of scenic shots and one of her standing next to a massive surfboard on the beach. She looks happy. The outdoor lifestyle obviously suits her. I head off to bed after half an hour of ogling Natalie Sawyer on Sky Sports News.

Mum's on the phone again bright and early Sunday morning. I'm fresher than normal, less hungover, but that doesn't stop her launching into her standard concerned tirade. She asks about Amy. It's like a broken record. I explain, again, that I won't be seeing her anymore. It's amazing how attached she is to someone she had zero relationship with. She says she just wants me to be happy but I'm not sure how much of that is for her rather than me. She reels off a list of my failed relationships, which is always nice to hear. She never knew Ellie existed so at least she can't add her to it. She's banging on about my brother instead of my dad this time. She's never found wanting when it comes to finding ways to show me I've come up short in life.

To be fair to her it must be disappointing when the younger sibling's all settled down with a mansion in the suburbs and a high-flying wife already pumping out grandkids, while I'm still stumbling my way through life, one week at a time. I can't take the lecture anymore so I tell her I've met someone. I chuck Hannah's name in there. Tell her she works up in town, in finance. Mum's impressed. Starts talking about how I should have told her I'd met someone new. About how she doesn't want to put any pressure on but she'd love to meet her. Christ, she's already got a hat on order for the wedding by the sounds of it. Tuesday's date had better go well.

Chapter Thirty-one

The date with Hannah goes like a dream. I take the afternoon off work so I can get up to town in plenty of time. We meet outside London Bridge tube station at seven and walk down towards the river, past Tower Bridge. We stroll through some quaint cobbled streets towards a small clutch of restaurants along a quiet stretch of the Thames.

I did a fair bit of research and plumped for a little Italian restaurant, off the beaten track, with great reviews. It's quiet and intimate and from what the reviews say, it does a banging ravioli. Hopefully the warm glow of the restaurant and a couple of glasses of wine will help us shortcut back to the end of our last evening together, when Hannah was shoving her tongue down my throat. I order a decent bottle of Sauvignon Blanc. Girls always like that. It's a bit classier than your standard Pinot Grigio. Twenty-six pounds. Not even the cheapest one on the menu.

Some suitably authentic Italian staff rush about, ferrying freshly made pasta dishes around the room. The place has got a nice feel about it. The kind of restaurant people go to when they're on a grown up date. The kind of restaurant nice guys take girls to show them they're serious. We hold each other's gaze as we clink glasses. She apologises profusely for being so hard to get hold of since our first date. I brush it off. Everyone has their own busy lives I say, hopefully hiding the fact that the whole thing had been doing my head in since we'd first spoken. She tells me about work and what a nightmare it is at the moment. I nod and smile and do my best to look interested. I never have been able to get my head around why people do jobs like hers. It sounds dull as dishwater.

Talk turns to dating. She asks me coyly if I'm still on any of the dating sites. I take this as a good sign. She wouldn't care if I was on them still if she wasn't keen. My normal response here would be to tell her I'm on all of them, and have a couple of other dates lined up for the weekend. Keep her on her toes. The old *treat them mean and keep them keen* mentality, which has never let me down in the past. But that's not really in keeping with the whole nice guy angle. I need to play this one a little bit differently. I need to make her see that I'm not just trying to get into her knickers. That I'm in the market for something serious.

I tell her I'm not on any of them anymore. That I've deleted all my accounts. I tell her that I like her and want to see what happens between us first. That I haven't been on any other dates since we first started talking. I'm pleased with my response. It's a good way to approach the situation. Mature. Lay my cards on the table. Let her know that I'm not someone who's going to mess her about by dating loads of women at the same time. She smiles at me. I'm pretty sure I nailed it.

She's still a member on firstdates.com apparently, but hasn't logged in for a couple of weeks. She barely even had time to reply to my text messages so I can believe that. She doesn't give much else away. As long as she's not got half of London auditioning to be her boyfriend that's ok with me. After tonight I reckon I'm in good shape. The wine continues to flow, as well as the conversation. It gets to ten-thirty and she tells me she needs to make a move. Month end isn't finished yet and she's got another long day ahead of her tomorrow.

A big reason I picked the restaurant was because of the location, which means we have to take a stroll along the river on the way back to the station. There's an evening mist hanging over the river, pierced by the lights of the buildings on the opposite bank and the illuminations decorating Tower Bridge. It's about as romantic a walk as you could hope for on a Tuesday night. I use the dropping temperature as an excuse to drape an arm around her shoulder as casually as I can manage. It's a very 'couply' thing to do so early on but I think it's in keeping with this new nice guy approach. The romantic stroll reaches its conclusion at London Bridge station. It's done the trick nicely. She pulls me in close and kisses me lustily. We're entangled for a good couple of minutes before she slips away down the escalators onto the central line back out to west London. A few months ago I would have scoffed at the idea of going on a third date if I hadn't had got any action from the first two, but now I curse myself for not asking if she was free this weekend. I need to get that locked in. A girl that kisses like that will be dynamite in the sack.

I get home to find Chris still up. He asks me how it went. Like he's some dating master now he's got Ruby and I'm the one in need of support. It winds me up a bit to be honest. I tell him it went well. That I'll be tucking into her in no time, once I've got the third date sorted out. A message from Hannah pops up:

Hey Danny, I just got home. Thanks so much for another amazing night, I loved every minute of it x

Only one kiss, but she had been devouring my face about an hour ago, so I don't read too much into it. Maybe this nice guy angle really is the way to go. Hannah's classy, fit, intelligent and definitely keen.

I text her on my way to the office the next day about the weekend, see if I can persuade her to let me cook her dinner one night. The day's a blur of viewings and chasing the solicitor for an update on the O'Shea sale. Nick wants it done as soon as possible so he can get the builders lined up and working as soon as the old dear's vacated the premises. He's changed his mind about letting her stay once he's bought it off her. Not that he's actually told her that, doesn't want any spanners in the works at this late stage. Nick's aiming to have it turned around and rented out within two weeks to six Polish lads he's already lined up. He might be a millionaire but he's not the type to miss out on a couple of grand a month's rent.

Chapter Thirty-two

Mrs Baker's place completes on the Friday morning. I walk her back to the car after she's dropped the keys off in the office. She's got a baggy grey tracksuit on. No make-up. Hair scraped up on top of her head. The glamour of a month ago has evaporated along with her marriage. Her car is full to the brim with cushions, pillows, toasters and kettles. The sort of loose crap people don't bother putting in a removal van. Somewhere buried beneath the duvets are her two kids. One of them pokes his head out and looks at me. He's crying. I close the door for her once she climbs back into the front seat. "I'm sorry," is all I can think to mouth to her through the closed window. She shrugs. One of her kids stares at me as her car crawls out of the car park. I need a drink.

Her sale takes us past last year's total, a record since the company started. David takes us all down the pub to celebrate. He even gets his credit card out. Christ, he must be due a hell of a bonus. Even Colin's in high spirits, despite having sold absolutely fuck all the entire year. David does a little speech thanking us for all the hard work. He can't help but ruin it by reminding us that there's still two weeks left in the financial year, and he expects to see some more sales coming in. He mentions the leaderboard, and the bonus coming down to whether the sale of Mrs O'Shea's property goes through in time. It fucking better, I really need that five grand. I grin at Charlie but he's too busy chatting up Alice to notice. He's been helping her a lot recently and her sales have really picked up. I wonder if this new bird he's been seeing knows how cosy he is with Alice.

By eight we're all pretty pissed. I'm stuck next to Colin who's banging on about some book he's reading. A fucking book. Jesus Christ hasn't he ever heard of TV. David's had a few as well, keeps telling me I've got a bright future if I can just iron out my rough edges. Cheeky prick. I made three times the cash he did last year.

Alice has cornered Charlie, fluttering her eye-lashes and flashing her cleavage at him. She's looking decent to be fair to her. Although that might be the beer. I've had at least eight pints. I interrupt them by asking Charlie if he wants another pint. Someone's got to step in or he'll end up banging her again and regretting it in the morning. He declines, his eyes searching for something somewhere down Alice's top. I let it go and head over to the bar. I get him a beer anyway and plonk it down in front of him, breaking the force-field between his eyes and her tits. I put it down a bit too firmly and some of the beer escapes the glass, splashing Alice's tight grey skirt. She gets the hump and heads off to powder her jugs or something in the toilets.

"What's up?" asks Charlie.

"Just doing you a favour," I say.

"A favour? What do you mean?"

"Look mate," I say, "you've got a bird now. You can't go sticking your dick in some dozy slag like Alice and ruining it." He tries to interrupt but I talk over him. "Don't get me wrong, she's got a great rack on her, but her face is average at best. She's probably a dirty bitch in the sack granted, and maybe after a few beers I'd give her one if, *if*, it was from behind and I didn't have to hear her talking, but do yourself a favour mate, don't do it." He looks at me for a minute or so but doesn't say anything. I must have hit the mark.

Alice comes back from the toilets. She's still in a mood by the looks of it. She picks her jacket up and says to Charlie, "Shall we go babe? We've got to be on the early train in the morning if we're going to get to my parents' in time for lunch."

He looks at me but doesn't say anything. Just grabs his coat and heads out the door with Alice. His girlfriend. Fuck. I didn't see that coming.

I get woken up about midnight by some kind of tapping. At first I think it's someone in the flat below putting some pictures up or something, which would be a fucking liberty at this time of night. I get up and put my ear to the floor. Nothing. I pad around the room in silence. It's coming from the room next door. Chris's room. Ruby's staying round. They've been out on some romantic dinner up in town. Fuck's sake, they're shagging. The tapping's insistent. Gentle. Like the wind delicately tapping a tree branch on the window. It occurs to me that they aren't even fucking. They're making love. Jesus Christ. He's probably got candles around the room and everything.

I check my phone. No reply from Hannah. Month end must have finished by now, so her work should have quietened down a bit. Maybe she's lost her phone? Maybe she didn't get my message about the weekend? I turn my phone off and try to go back to sleep.

I'm down the pub, getting on it with the lads when Hannah finally replies. Three fucking days after I messaged her. She's not going to be around for a few weeks so she'll give me a shout when she's free again. I've been on the other end of enough messages like that to know what it means. The worst kind of generic, vague brush off. I read it a couple of times, knowing full well that I won't hear from her again.

This nice guy thing is bullshit. This is what you end up with when you take a girl out properly. When you make an effort. Do the couply thing. Listen to what she's got to say. Don't try and get into her pants the first time you meet her. You get the piss taken out of you, that's what. Why stick your tongue down someone's throat if you aren't keen on them? Why gush about what a great time you had on a date if you don't want to do it again? I'm raging, so I head to the bar and get a round of shots in. It's only two in the afternoon but fuck it. And fuck her. And fuck being nice.

"Wahey," shouts Gaz when I bring the tray of shots and plonk them on the table, "up for a big night are we?"

We sling them back and I go to get more. Every round from then on is a beer and shot. Vodka, Tequila, Jaegar, Sambuca all make an appearance. We're heading for oblivion tonight. Via Inferno's, obviously. All of us are slurring by the time we get in there. I look around at the same old shit. The same dickhead doorman with his little rope outside, judging people's suitability to enter like he isn't the least qualified on the face of the fucking planet to do so. The same arseholes behind the bar who somewhere along the line mistook the ability to mix a drink as an excuse to strut about like rock stars. Preening behind the bar like they're the masters of the universe, not pricks with dodgy facial hair charging twelve quid for a glorified rum and coke. The same moronic girls standing around, painted oak with fake tan and make-up, dressed up with their tits hanging out on the off-chance of spreading their legs for a lower league footballer. Or an electrician pretending to be one. Worst of all I see the same hordes of blokes hovering around the outskirts of the dancefloor. Packs of hyenas waiting to pick off the girls weak or stupid enough to buy their bullshit.

And we're all part of it. Me, Gaz, Ben and Ritz. Not Charlie though. He slipped out of all of this while I wasn't looking. He'll be shacked up with that pair of tits with a face, Alice, within a couple of months at this rate. No, fuck this place. I storm out of there after only half an hour.

I stumble down the high street, trying to chat a couple of birds up, but getting nowhere. I message Michelle, to see if she's around. I feel like everything's got on top of me a bit. Like I've got myself into a bit of a rut. I need someone to help me out of it. She messages back. She's been on a few dates with someone. She's off the market. Fuck's sake. I stumble the twenty minute walk home while I frantically scroll through my options on Tinder. There's one: Donna. She's made up to hear from me and asks if I want to go out this week. I find myself saying yes, despite the fact I know I'm not really interested, and I'm pretty sure I won't fancy her, because I realise in a moment of panic there's no one else.

Chapter Thirty-three

I know immediately that I don't fancy Donna. She turns up for our Tuesday night date and I feel something sink inside me. It's an instinctive reaction so it's not my fault.

She's obviously put the most photogenic pictures she can find on her dating profile, which pisses me off. She's at least a stone heavier than her photos and has that slightly bloated face people who spend a lot of their time drinking have. Like someone is slowly, but relentlessly, inflating her head like a balloon. She's also got that rosy tint people who spend most of the week inhaling alcohol tend to get. I suspect the last couple of years have been hard on Donna's liver. I toy with the idea of making an excuse and bailing out, but she's not *that* bad. I mean, she's not as fit as Hannah, Amy, Ellie, Michelle, Sophie or even Emma from school, but she's alright.

Besides, it's not like I've got plenty of options on the table at the moment, and maybe after a couple of drinks I'll get a shag out of it.

We chat on the way to the pub and have a bit of a laugh. She's already had a quick glass of wine on the way. Nerves apparently. We find our way into a rammed pub somewhere near Clapham North Station. It's an absolute sweat box. Standing at the bar being jostled by groups of blokes is not the best place for a first date, but fortunately a young couple stand up to leave just as we're wondering whether to find somewhere else. Donna quickly dashes to the free table, shouting to me over her shoulder to get her a large glass of Merlot. She gets there in the nick of time, just before a group of braying rugby types nab it to down pints of piss or touch each other's knobs, or whatever it is that rugby lads do.

We settle down at the table, clink our glasses together, and begin the ritualistic dating small talk. What we do for work, where we live, where we grew up. All that shite you have to do when you first meet someone. She does some kind of marketing that she seems to think is life or death important, but I struggle to understand what she actually does. She keeps saying the word *branding*, like it answers all of my questions and stops the need for any other explanation. She's big into going out with the girls and bangs on about going to some place called The Ship in Clapham every Sunday. It sounds fucking horrendous. An absolute shit-fight. I'm about halfway through my pint as Donna sinks the dregs of her glass of wine. Not wanting to leave her with an empty glass, I ask her if she wants another. She nearly bites my hand off.

"Shall we do some shots as well," she suggests with what I think is an attempt at a cheeky wink. Why not, I think. If I'm going to shag her I'm going to need to be pissed.

"Two Jagerbombs coming up" I say.

An hour in, I've done three pints in a vain attempt to keep up with Donna's four glasses of red. She is absolutely throwing them down. The midlands twang that I noticed at the start of the date has gradually been lost in amongst her general slurring. She stands up, announces she's off to *drain the weasel*, and totters off across the room, making a beeline for the bathrooms, her heels clicking the along the stone floor as she goes. She turns a few heads, which gives her even more confidence.

Unfortunately for her, the looks aren't as flattering as she thinks. She's a bit of a state and slightly stumbles as she reaches the bathroom doors. She returns a few minutes later, clutching two more shots she's acquired on her way back. "I got these for free," she squeals excitedly, "I had to give the barman a peck on the cheek to get them, but a free shot's a free shot."

I force down the shot, but by now I'm pretty sure I'm not going to shag the drunken mess sitting in front of me. Somehow, I manage to grind my way through until nearly ten o'clock, by which point Donna has started to resemble an angry Ronald McDonald, with red wine and lipstick smeared around her lips. I idly wonder if she's annoying because she's shit-faced or if it's just her personality.

She leans in conspiratorially and says, "I think I might be a little bit tipsy." She points at me across the table. "It's only because I haven't eaten anything. It was ungentlemanly of you to not buy me dinner," she slurs across the table. Her finger is uncomfortably close to my face. "The man should always buy the girl dinner on the first date." She leans back into her chair and downs the rest of her wine in one enormous gulp, completely oblivious to the fact that she is the perfect example of why I never go out for dinner on a first date.

Mercifully, the manager comes to my rescue by coming over to our table and telling us that he won't be serving Donna any more drink, because she's had too much. As I feared, Donna doesn't take this with good grace.

"We were just leaving anyway," she slurs at him. "It's shit in here." She says this at a volume that causes a few tables in the immediate vicinity to turn round and watch the unfolding spectacle. "Come on, let's get out of here," she says as she stomps off. For a split second I think about hiding in the toilets, under the table, or just behind a massive rugby bloke standing at the bar, but with all eyes on me I slink out after her, staring at the floor as I go. I'm frantically thinking up an excuse, any excuse, to put an end to the night and get the fuck away from her as I follow her outside, but it turns out I don't need one. The oxygen has hit Donna's brain in the thirty seconds she's been outside and she's already emptying the contents of her stomach up against some poor local resident's front door. "I think I may have drunk a little bit too much," she says between retches, her outstretched palms keeping her upright as she sprays an unholy amount of liquid all over the place.

I weigh up my options. I could just run off. It won't make any difference as I'll never have to see again. Luckily for her there's a taxi rank opposite us so I do the decent thing and walk her to it. There's no queue because it's only about ten o'clock. We shuffle over towards the first cab. Donna stinks of puke. Her eyes are bleary and red. She disgusts me. The cab driver wants fifty quid 'insurance' money in case she pukes in his car. I negotiate him down to thirty while she's already dozing in the back of the cab, her mouth agape and tongue lolling around.

It's only a ten minute walk back to the flat. I grab myself a burger on the way. I'm concerned. Donna's a flailing drunk, desperately trying to grab hold of anyone who'll have her. Frantically trying to make sure she's not left on the shelf while everyone else pairs up. But she's only a year older than me and I went on a date with her because I don't have any other options. The worrying thought occurs to me that maybe I'm closer to being left on the shelf than I ever realised.

Chapter Thirty-four

I go through the motions at work for the next couple of days. All I care about is getting Mrs O'Shea's property sold to Nick. I ignore everything else. I dodge phone calls and viewings and continually hound the solicitors. I need that money. The three grand from Nick and the five grand bonus. Eight fucking grand. Everything will feel better with a big lump of cash in the bank. They call me back eventually, just to shut me up. We finally have a date. The exchange and completion will happen on the same day, Wednesday next week. Two days before the end of financial year deadline. Fucking fantastic. I go to the pub to celebrate. On my own.

Alice is bringing in packed lunches for Charlie now so he's stopped going down the pub. They go off and sit in the park like a couple of teenagers. I don't mention the completion date to him yet. He'll choke on his cheese and pickle sandwiches when he finds out I've pipped him to the post. I do three Stellas, just to take the edge off the rest of the afternoon.

"You coming along to the bowling night tonight?" asks Charlie when I get back to the office.

I look at him, incredulous. He has got to be fucking kidding.

"You've got to be fucking kidding?" I say.

"No, we thought we'd go along. You should come. It'll be a laugh."

It won't be a laugh. At all. It'll be shit. But the truth is, what the fuck else am I going to do tonight. Sit like a spare part in my own flat while Chris and Ruby entwine themselves together on my sofa. I note Charlie used the term *we*, obviously referring to him and Alice. How very fucking cosy.

"The *royal we* now is it now?" I ask. He glows like a radioactive beetroot and scuttles off back to his desk. I realise that they're all leaving at four tonight for the bowling. The extra hour out of the office swings it and I agree to tag along.

David hangs a sign on the door saying *closed early for team night out*. Jesus. We all have to squeeze into one cab, as he wants to keep down expenses. It's one of those hybrids. Good for the environment and all that. Unfortunately I'm sat next to Colin whose stink will burn a hole in the roof if we're in here too long. Then the ozone layer will really be in trouble. We spill out of the cab before it's even come to a halt outside the bowling alley. David mistakes our thirst for clean air for enthusiasm for the forced fun.

We exchange our shoes for those godawful half and halfs, which look ridiculous with my navy-blue Reiss suit. Charlie helps Alice into her shoes. He's acting like a twelve year old with his first hard-on.

"I'll get the drinks in," I say, heading straight for the bar. I'm going to need to get on it if I'm going to make it through this evening. I order four pints for the blokes and a large glass of Pinot for Alice. While I'm waiting for the twelve-year old behind the bar to pour them I sneak a double vodka and redbull down my neck. I carry over Alice's wine and two of the beers first, handing them to David and Colin. On my way back to collect the final two beers I have an idea.

"Stick a shot of vodka in that one mate," I say, pointing at the one I've earmarked for Charlie.

We cheers and clink our glasses together while David makes a half-arsed attempt to praise all our good work so far this year. Charlie grimaces as he takes his first sip, but blames the odd taste on the fact he cleaned his teeth just before we left the office. I make a mental note to get him a shot in the next one as well. David's best attempt at banter is to give us all hilarious nicknames for the bowling. The scoreboard announces that Dangerous Dave's up first. He hurls both balls into the gutter and makes a joke about needing to warm up. I refuse to join in with everyone else's fake laughter.

We all score in the sevens or eights until Captain Colin steps up and nearly destroys the pins on his first go. This proves not to be a fluke as he proceeds to do the same with nine of his ten goes. It turns out Colin used to be a professional bowler. I'd have never have picked it. Towards the end of the game I switch targets and start putting vodka in his beer instead of Charlie's, but his aim never wavers. Impressive. He wins, obviously, but I wipe the floor with everyone else. Charlie's pissed from all the vodkas I've been sneaking into his beers, David's got the hand-eye coordination of a five year old, and Alice is a girl, so my second place is not something I'll be shouting too much about.

The evening dies a death after we finish our second game. Colin heads home to feed his cat. David's getting an earful from his enormous wife about being out past nine o'clock so has to shoot off. Charlie's not feeling too hot and disappears to the toilet for a lengthy comfort break. I slide across to sit next to Alice to see if I can build some bridges. She's a bottle of wine down by this point and slurring a little as she asks me about Charlie.

She's made an effort tonight. She scrubs up well to be fair to her. A bit of mascara here and a bit of blusher there has worked a treat. I've never really been up this close to her. She smells good. She's also wearing a particularly low-cut top. Alice may not be the brightest but she certainly knows how to use her assets. I shift my position to get a better look. She's got some kind of lacy bra on. She sees me looking and shifts away a couple of inches. "Where's Charlie?" she asks, looking around.

"At the bar chatting up some girl," I lie.

"No he's not, is he?" She asks uncertainly. She's obviously got it bad for the bloke. I let my lack of response hang in the air.

"What you doing after this?" I enquire as I move a touch closer again. Our legs brush against each other.

"Not sure. Going home I s'pose," she slurs.

"Do you fancy another drink?" I press my leg against hers again. This time I leave it there. Her legs are surprisingly hard. Toned even. Interesting. She'd never stuck me as the athletic type before. Maybe there's a good little body hiding under there after all. No wonder Charlie keeps going back.

"No, I've definitely had enough," she says. I'll be all over the place if I have another one."

"I'd like to see that." I counter. I let my hand touch her leg. I lean in a bit closer. Sneak another peek down her top. Those jugs look even bigger from here.

She moves my hand. "Don't," she says. "I'm with Charlie."

I move my hand back to her toned thigh. "You can do so much better than him," I whisper in her ear. "So much better."

She pushes me away, more forcefully this time and tells me again, louder, with more anger. "Get off me. I said I'm with Charlie."

"What's going on here?" asks Charlie who's chosen the worst possible moment to make his return from the toilet. Alice leaps to her feet and flings her arms around him.

"Just a misunderstanding," I say, holding my palms up in mock surrender, like a kid caught with his hand in the cookie jar.

"He was trying it on with me," she blurts out between sobs, "I told him we're together and he just kept trying."

I look at Charlie, my palms still up, defusing the situation, and realise that if anyone on this planet knows what I'm like with birds, it's him. Which means I've got zero chance of him believing my side of the story.

"Fuck off Danny," he spits as he puts his arm around her. "You can be a real dick sometimes." They storm off and head straight for the exit. I guess they really are together.

I order myself another pint at the bar but realise midway through the first sip that I'm already drunk, and am drinking on my own in a bowling alley. It doesn't feel like I've made much progress with getting out of that rut I'm in. I leave the beer and dial the only number I can think of that'll take my mind away from all of this shit.

Chapter Thirty-five

I'm banging away on Donna and I'd rather be anywhere else in the entire world. I'm in her dusty flat in Brixton and two of her three cats are watching me intently as I take out my worldly frustration on her. She doesn't seem to notice the audience. There's also a tortoise in the living room somewhere, slowly doing laps around her sofa. She introduced me to them all when I stumbled through her front door as if they were human beings. They all have real people's names. Her cats are called Billy, Joe and Sarah. Her tortoise is called Terence. She is totally off her rocker.

In the total absence of any other options I made my way over here in a cab from the bowling alley. There was no way I was spending another night in with just a wank-sock for company. She's been in all night having a Kardashian's marathon and eating hummus, so she jumped at the chance of my unexpected visit despite the fact I'd completely pied her off after our disastrous first date.

As I suspected, she was just as irritating sober. She wittered on for a full ten minutes about a new product she's doing a marketing strategy for. I pointed out that if the product was any good the company wouldn't need to spend millions of pounds convincing people to buy it but she just looked at me like I'd just shat on her carpet. It seemed pretty straightforward to me but she just launched into a monologue about how I only thought that because I didn't understand marketing. I couldn't be arsed with listening to the unbridled shite coming out of her mouth anymore so I went in for the kill and instigated the shagging as quickly as possible. I could tell it'd been a while for her by how quickly she whipped her clothes off and how quickly her hands went for my trousers.

It's been about half an hour since she said anything about marketing, mainly because her face is buried in one of her pillows. I can't really tell if she's enjoying herself from my vantage point behind her, but ultimately I don't give a shit. It's not essential to the success of this little interaction. It's more of a nice to have.

It's taking a bit of time so my mind wanders elsewhere while I keep up the rhythm, like a guitarist pounding out a chugging riff whilst singing a different melody over the top. Thoughts come and go while I bask in her muffled silence. I wonder what time on Wednesday Mrs O'Shea's house will go through. I wonder if Barrie and Aberdeen will put the five grand bonus in my next pay packet. I wonder how quickly Nick will drop my envelope full of cash round. Eight fucking grand. Result. I start to wonder what I'll do with it. Maybe two weeks in Marbella instead of one. Gaz and Ritz will definitely be keen for that, if they can scrape the money together. Ben won't have that problem; he'll just scrawl a couple of fake signatures on football shirts and sell them on Ebay. I could potentially have even longer off. Quit the office and head over to Thailand. Apparently they've got some unreal bars over there in Bangkok and Phuket. And the full moon parties on the islands look proper mental.

I wonder what Ellie's doing over in Australia. Probably the same as Donna here, getting railed into next week, just by a bloke with more tattoos and longer hair. Maybe I'll go and visit her with the money. I wonder what Amy's doing. She's probably with her new boyfriend. Cuddling and spooning and falling asleep while holding hands. All the stuff I wouldn't let her do.

I've been pumping away on Donna for the best part of forty minutes and I can't be arsed to carry on. I pretend to finish and roll off of her. Her bloated, red, scarecrow of a face comes up, gasping, from the pillow. I feel disgusting.

"That was amazing," she says, in between deep breaths. I don't reply. I just stare at the ceiling. I give it a few minutes before I check the time. It's nearly one in the morning. "I'd better be going," I say, "I've got to be in the office early in the morning." She's not happy with that at all. Says she feels like I've just used her for sex. Which I have. I guess she was expecting some hand-holding or spooning afterwards. Something I've noticed about sex over the last few weeks is that it's left me feeling totally hollow. Has it always been like that and I've just not noticed? Here I am lying next to someone I've just been intimate with and I'd give anything to be anywhere else. I feel like my insides have been emptied out. I don't even bother trying to fake warmth and emotion.

I realise I'll do anything to get out of her flat as quickly as possible, so I just put on my clothes and go. "I'll call you," I say as I go to the door, leaving her lying on the bed, naked, one of her cats covering her modesty. I realise I probably will call her as well. When I reach rock bottom again. Probably sometime soon.

A blast of cold air wash over me as I step back out into the night. I feel like walking home. It's a fair old trek, probably about forty minutes, but I need some air and a bit of space. The biting wind chases the alcohol from my blood. I think about the Bakers. About her having to move back in with her parents in her mid-forties, betrayed by the bloke who was supposed to be looking after her. About the kids, snivelling in an unfamiliar house, not knowing what's going on, or why their dad isn't there anymore. I see Mr Baker's dead eyes again. He'll have moved into the studio flat now, which probably would have taken about ten minutes. Did he feel as empty as I do when he shagged that au pair? Did he do it just to see if he still could? Was it worth the risk? Throwing everything away for a quick poke.

Amy pops back into my head again. I'm angry, but not at her. I chased her away. Like Mr Baker did. I was too busy looking for somewhere else to put my attention. Just because I wanted to make sure I still could. Too busy looking around to see what was under my nose. I check her Facebook. She's deleted me now so I can only see her profile picture. It's been changed since I last looked. It's a picture of her and that guy I tried to punch. The one who laid me out. They're at a wedding or something. I can't look at it anymore. It makes me feel even worse.

I check Ellie's Instagram. She's still having a great time over in Australia by the looks of it. Loads of pictures of her doing exciting stuff. Bungee jumping, sky diving, snorkelling. In every picture she's surrounded by blokes. I bet they're all having a pop at her. I've got all this shit with Charlie as well now. He seems happy with Alice. I was out of order there. I can't even explain why I did that really.

The flat's silent when I get home. I assume Chris is staying at Ruby's. I sit down on the sofa and put the TV on. I don't really feel like going to bed yet. There's some awful American show on about the apocalypse. The sort of shit that gets shown at nearly two in the morning. All the characters are suspicious of each other and I can't really work out who the good guys are and who are the bad. Maybe they're all kind of both. I wake up on the sofa with dribble down my shirt sometime around five and manage to scrape myself from the living room into bed for the last couple of hours sleep before I have to be up for work again.

Chapter Thirty-Six

The office is a ghost town when I get in. I'm clutching a steak slice and an orange Lucozade and my head feels like it's going to explode. David's the only one here. To be fair I'd spend my whole life in the office if my wife looked like his. Alice and Charlie have both taken the day off, probably to spend it spooning or skipping through a meadow or something.

Part of me is glad they aren't here, it'd be awkward as hell, but I can't get the apology out of the way until I see them so that's a bit annoying. I consider texting Charlie but it feels like something I should do in person. David doesn't mess about and bombs it straight over as soon as I'm at my desk. I've got a mouthful of Ginster's finest and he's already blabbering about some meeting with the bosses. I'd nearly forgotten, they always do this at the end of the year. Make a big song and dance about the top salesman.

Frankly, I'm too hungover for it today, but he's very insistent and puts me straight in a cab. Another bloody hybrid. The bastard cab driver won't even let me eat my steak slice so I have to chuck half of it away. At least the bloke's got the blower on full blast, which starts to shift some of my hangover.

All this official bollocks is a bit unnecessary really. I would've been happy with an email. Or maybe one of those printed certificates. An audience with the big bosses seems a bit over the top. Especially as there's still a week or so until the end of the year. Nick's purchase of the O'Shea place isn't completely over the line. But I guess I'm about to smash the record for sales this year, so they're probably just getting a bit ahead of themselves, what with all the cash I'm pulling in for them. At least I can ask them how soon I'll get my bonus.

"Take a seat," says the girl on reception as I arrive, "they'll be ready for you shortly."

She's a solid eight. Maybe an eight and a half. Dark brown eyes with her almost black hair cut into a hard fringe. She's a bit too covered up for my liking, so I can't tell what she's packing in the tit department. I toy with the idea of giving her some chat. I try to catch her eye but she doesn't look up for the entire ten minutes I'm sitting there. I look around the room. They've done their best to make the place plush. Pictures of generic developments from around the world all over the walls. There's a hotel in Dubai, a new build in Asia somewhere, a resort in Italy. There's a green plant on every available surface. All attempts to paper over the fact I'm sitting in a pokey space above a car showroom on an industrial estate, with only one window and a view over the car repair yard behind us.

"The partners will see you now," she says, buzzing me in and gesturing to the door. She's got absolutely zero banter, which is a shame. A real waste. I step inside a large room with an oval table that seats about twenty; the boardroom. The two partners sit on the opposite side of the table and gesture for me to take a seat. It's like some dreadful corporate episode of the X-Factor. Which I guess is what The Apprentice is, thinking about it. For a celebratory meeting the mood is grim. There aren't even any custard creams.

I try to up the energy level. "How is everybody?" I ask as I take my seat. The question hangs in the air, unanswered. Miserable bastards.

"Mr Small," begins Aberdeen, who has prime position at the centre of the table, directly opposite me, "you've been with us just under a year now, correct?" He's shuffling some papers in front of him. I can't make out what they are from my side of the table.

"Yep," I say. Christ are they always this glum? I've just made the fuckers a shitload of money and they're both sitting there chewing on shit sandwiches.

"I've got your application form in front of me," he says, which is a bit strange. Not the obvious lead into a slap on the back and a five grand bonus cheque. "If you were to fill this out again, is there anything you might fill in differently?" He slides the application form across to me. It feels a bit hot in here. The collar of my shirt feels tight. Like I've accidentally bought the wrong size and now it's starting to choke me. The hangover sweats are kicking in, and my stomach's rumbling like dodgy washing machine.

My application form. It's a straight up ambush and I know the game's up. I study it closely. So closely. Closer than I ever studied it when I was filling the fucking thing out. I gaze at it in the vague hope that the offending part of the form, the bit I know he's talking about, might disappear if I stare at it for long enough.

The bit that asks the question: 'Have you ever been convicted of a criminal offence?'

The bit where I lied and ticked no.

My brain scrabbles around frantically searching for a solution but comes up short. I decide to play it straight. See if I can talk my way out of it.

"Er, yeah, maybe there's a couple of bits I'd maybe fill out differently now, given the chance," I say, casually, like we're just chatting in a bar.

"Which bits might they be?" asks Aberdeen. I get the distinct impression he's enjoying watching me squirm. He doesn't take his beady little eyes off me for a second.

"Maybe the bit about the criminal record," I offer, grinning as sheepishly as I can, in the hope they'll see the funny side of the situation. I'm the top salesman at the company for fuck's sake. I make them a fortune. Surely they'll turn a blind eye. But how they react all depends on how much they know. Which really depends on how much whoever's grassed me up has told them.

"Why don't you tell us what happened?" he says.

I need to get them onside. Get some sympathy. Sway things my way. So I go for the emotional approach. "It was a long time ago," I say. "I was going through a difficult time. I'd just had a very difficult break up."

I pause, to let that sink in. To let them know how tough it all was on me.

"Go on," says Aberdeen. He's not prepared to let me slip into full story-telling mode. He's business-like. Blunt and emotionless. Like a fucking robot.

"My girlfriend had just left me and I didn't take it very well."

"Didn't take it very well?" chimes in Barrie, his eyebrow raised.

"She walked out on my birthday. She wouldn't return my calls or messages. I just wanted to try to fix it. I wanted to make her understand that whatever the problem was we could work through it somehow. But she wouldn't even speak to me. We were young and passionate. I didn't let her go easily. In the end it was all totally blown out of proportion. It was just a load of phone calls from someone desperate to speak to his girlfriend."

"Surely you wouldn't have been arrested for harassment for just a couple of phone calls?" Barrie again. He obviously knows about the charge. He thinks he's a right smart prick.

"Ok, there were a couple of times I went to her flat as well. But I know that was wrong. Like I say, I was having a hard time coming to terms with it. I was drinking a lot and everything just got a bit out of control. I regret it all now."

"So you got charged with harassment. What happened?"

I may as well fess up. They know the details, of this bit of the story at least.

"I spent six months at Wandsworth Open Prison."

There it is. Out in the open. All my cards on the table. I feel deflated. Like I'm three inches smaller suddenly. They both stare at me like I'm some sort of pond life. It was a long time ago. I'm the top sales guy. Surely they'll let it slide. They'd be chucking a fortune away if they got rid of me.

"The thing is," says Barrie, who's really revelling in this now, "six months seems a very heavy punishment for a few phone calls and a harassment charge." He's fishing for more info but I stare at him. Poker face. Giving him nothing.

He leans in for the money shot, "But that's not all it was, was it?"

And I know I'm sunk. Worst of all I know who's sunk me.

Chapter Thirty-seven

I was an idiot back in those days. A soppy dickhead. I got sucked by a girl like some teenage loser. I said things like *I love you.* We called each other stupid little nicknames like *babes* and *sweets*. We were one of those annoying couples you see that gaze at each other like they're the only people in the entire fucking world. We met in the second year of Uni. We were young but we talked a lot about the future, about kids and marriage and travelling the world together as if our relationship was never going to end. Like they always do.

Everything stopped the first time I saw her. It was like some kind of Disney film where everything else moved in slow motion. She said when I'd first spoken to her, when I was drunk enough to attempt a stab at confidence, that it was like I had a glow around me, that she couldn't see anything else in the entire room. The person I'd been for the previous two years disappeared there and then. No more excessive boozing, drugs and late night booty calls. I just wanted to be around her. All the time. She was perfect.

We spent every night together, her small frame nestled perfectly into my arms. She said I made her feel safe. I'd walk through the streets of Bournemouth at two in the morning, through the rivers of puke and piss and god knows what in the back streets, to meet her at the end of her shift at a late night bar in the town centre. Her mates marvelled at what a gentleman her boyfriend was. At how dedicated he was to her. But it was bullshit really. I was just a scared kid, terrified that one of the B-list celebrities or lower league footballers queuing up to try and take her away from me every night at the bar would finally succeed. That their money and clothes and arrogance would finally chip away at her resilience. My terror masqueraded conveniently as devotion. I was a fraud.

Towards the end of our final year in Bournemouth we endlessly talked about our plans. She wanted to stay there, amongst the bars and clubs and carefree rhythm that seemed to lap in with the waves on the beach. I wasn't so sure, the place seemed a bit empty and superficial to me. Full of forty-year olds in clubs wearing sunglasses and leather jackets, clinging on to a youth that had long since left them behind. But I would have followed her into the sea if that's what she'd wanted. We settled on a different plan; to travel Central and South America together. It was exciting and romantic and it meant we could put off having to make any other decisions. We made it through the stress of final exams. I talked her down from her panic the night before one of the biggest ones. It's amazing how important they seemed at the time, when in reality no one in the real world gives two shits about your exam results.

We both passed. We both graduated. Our parents met at the graduation ceremony. They sat next to each other, amongst thousands of other parents gawping at their kids, dressed as tosspots in a big hall near the sea front. My dad even made the effort to be there. She was the first girlfriend that'd ever met him. The chapter closed on that part of our life together. I couldn't wait for the next part to begin. Like a numpty I'd ordered guide book after guide book. Brazil on a shoestring. The Mayan Trails of Guatemala. Diving in Honduras. I spent hours poring over every conceivable trip idea on the Lonely Planet website.

It turned out she had different ideas. The day after graduation she announced she wanted some time apart. She still had feelings for me but wanted to be single for a while. To find herself. To take some time to get to know what she wanted from life. Alone. I left Bournemouth the next day, after three hours on her doorstep, tearfully begging her to reconsider, while my saint of a mother waited patiently round the corner, her car full of my worldly possessions.

Apparently time apart still meant she wanted me to come down to Bournemouth and stay with her every Saturday night, so I dutifully sat on the train every Saturday morning and Sunday night. She told me she loved me every time I saw her, which just led to more floods of confused tears. The torture continued for six months until something hardened inside of me, like a pathway running through the centre of me, the bit capable of love and affection had been paved over. With tarmac. It occurred to me that she was mugging me off. That she was taking the chronic piss. That the only thing that had changed in our relationship was that I'd somehow given her permission to fuck other people while I sat at home wondering what she was going, waiting for her to realise she'd made a mistake.

The tearful calls were replaced by angry outbursts. Raging abusive voicemails and spiteful texts at all times of day and night. I fuelled the rage with coke and alcohol. Told her I knew what she was up to. That I could see who she really was now. That I finally saw the real her. I replaced her with a string of others. Interchangeable names and faces who pushed the memory of her away, minute by minute, night by night. She ignored my messages, my phone calls and voicemails, my pathetic, unsuccessful attempts to fuck her mates. She ignored my vengeance which only stoked it further.

After a particularly heavy weekend, during which I'm sure I continued my hate campaign, I received a knock on the door; the Police. Did I know anything about the complaints of harassment she'd made against me? The fucking cheek of it. She'd mugged me right off, was probably fucking every bloke in Bournemouth and yet she had the balls to complain when I told her what I thought about it. The coppers were alright to be fair. Just a couple of young lads. They understood what was going on, they knew where I was coming from. They told me just to cool it for a bit. To lay off saying anything that could be deemed to be a threat and it'd all blow over. They even shook my hand on the way out.

Obviously I wasn't having that. At all. The bitch had mugged me off all over again. I was fucking furious. Decided it was time to go give her something else to think about. I started off small by sending a couple of nice pictures she'd sent me back in the day to a couple of our mutual mates. Just a few lads we both knew. She had a cracking pair of tits, so it seemed a shame not to share them around. I had a great collection of photos of her so in the end I started up a little group on Facebook. It ended up with about four hundred blokes on it, all leering over naked pictures of her. Some of them even started making requests.

She ended up finding out about it. Called me up in tears. Begged me to take them down. Saying if I'd ever cared about her at all I'd stop. While she was pleading on the phone I posted the cherry on top. One of our own private videos. She cried. I laughed. Maybe she should have thought about all this before she mugged me off.

I got another knock at the door the next day. One of the copper lads again. This time he had some lezzer with him. A real bulldog. Right fired up she was. I could tell she wanted to clump me one straight away. Free speech I argued, but she couldn't wait to nick me and take me down the station. Fucking political correctness and all that bollocks. The lad with her looked embarrassed about the whole thing. I ended up going down for six months. The judge said he wanted to make an example of people like me. What a fucking joke. I couldn't believe it. Prison was a piece of piss. I just played a load of Playstation and pool. But not a day went by when I didn't think about what she'd done to me. I wish I'd never met the bitch. Just goes to show you, you can't say anything these days if you're a bloke. Always some feminist waiting to take offence and grass you up.

Chapter Thirty-eight

The wankers sent me straight home after the meeting, told me not to go back into the office until David had been in touch. Once they'd worked out their *next course of action*, whatever that means. Ungrateful pricks. I've made them a fortune this year and they get shitty about one little thing like this.

I resolve to find the positive in the whole situation though, as there's nothing quite like an unexpected day off. It's like a snow day when you're at school or waking up to realise it's a bank holiday that you'd forgotten all about. I take my trousers off as soon as I walk in the door. It's not a proper day off if you don't spend it in your pants. My shirt and tie are quickly replaced by a t-shirt from an old mate's stag do a couple of years back. It's got a picture of an absolute whale of a bird he shagged back in the day on the front of it and *pussy magnets on tour* on the back. Classic stuff. Magaluf had no idea what hit it that weekend. Fucking brilliant it was. I don't see those boys much anymore; they're all boring as fuck with wives and kids now. I'm glad I've got Marbella with the lads to look forward to. Should be great banter.

I have a lazy mooch on Tinder and fire out a few lines to see what bites. I get a couple of messages back. They're not that fit, which means getting them to put out will be easy, so I keep them on the hook in case nothing better comes up.

David calls at about eleven. He's got his official voice on, a bit like when my mum's on the phone pretending to be posh. He starts blathering about professional standards and company reputation.

"Hold on a second," I say, a grim realisation creeping over me, "what are you saying David?"

He pauses. "After careful consideration the board have decided that you don't adhere to the standards Barrie and Aberdeen expect from their employees. Our legal team feel that the fact you lied about your criminal record is grounds enough for immediate dismissal. Next week's wages will be your final pay."

I don't say anything for a moment as it sinks in.

"You're fired, basically," he says with barely concealed satisfaction.

"Wait," I say, scrabbling, "I've made a fortune for you fuckers this year." He doesn't reply. "What about my sales bonus? I earnt that fair and square."

"The board feels," he says, not bothering to cover up his glee, "that as the financial year doesn't end until next week, you will not be eligible for the bonus. It'll go to the *employee of the company* with the most sales. You are no longer an employee."

Fucking Charlie. He grassed me up and now he's taking my money. The absolute fucking state of it. "That's my five grand," I shout, raging.

"No Danny," he says, "it's not." The prick actually has the balls to hang up on me.

I phone Charlie. The fucking grass. He doesn't pick up. Another horrific thought occurs to me. I dial Nick's number. He picks up on the first ring. "Danny," he says, "what the hell's been going on?" Not even a hello. I tell him the lay of the land. That I've been stitched up. That I'm out the door. That there might be a bit of delay in the O'Shea deal while I get myself a job at another estate agent's. That it should only take a couple of weeks.

"Don't worry about the O'Shea deal," he says, "Charlie's dealing with it. I'll still be going through Barrie and Aberdeen. He called me this morning while you were in your meeting. We're going ahead as planned on Wednesday."

"But what about my fee?" I shout, "That's my money. You owe me." He hangs up. Fuck. I call him back. Three times in a row. He doesn't answer. Fuck. *Fuck.* FUCK.

I phone Charlie again. No answer. He has well and truly fucked me here.

I look at the time. Half-eleven. Fuck it, I need a drink. I suck back the only can of Stella left in the fridge. It's not enough. I sling on my jeans and trainers on and head down to the Falcon. The dickhead behind the bar riles me up even further by making me wait until the dot of twelve before he'll serve me any alcohol. I have to sit there while he stares at the clock, his hand on the pump. I go straight for the Stella. I've sunk three by one o'clock. I try Charlie again. No answer. The cunt's ignoring me. He can't hide forever. I know where he lives for a start. I get a Sambuca with the next beer. I'm swimming in alcohol and rage now and I need an outlet.

I get on Tinder again. No more replies. Just the birds from earlier. I ask them both what they're doing tonight. One of them, Kat, is a total waste of space. Won't come over to mine, says she doesn't know anything about me. Probably a fucking feminist or something. She's not fit anyway. I send her a picture of my cock for a laugh, then block her. The other one, Alex, is easy to persuade, despite the fact she says she'd prefer to meet for drinks first. She's actually semi-attractive so that's a result. I give her my address and she agrees to come round at eight once I make it clear that going out for drinks is not an option.

I leave another message for Charlie, this time on his office phone. The barman refuses me another round and suggest I have a shandy instead, like I'm some sort of homo. I tell him to go fuck himself and head over the road to the Clapham North, almost getting hit by a fucking Korean in a giant car she can barely control in the process. I assume she's Korean because there's fucking loads of them round here, but it could be any of them really, I'm fucked if I can tell the difference. I need to ease off a bit now I've sorted out a bird to come over later so I move onto Kronenburg. I have a couple but start to feel fuzzy and bloated. I need a walk to clear my head.

    I stumble a bit along the pavement and end up outside the office. David and his paedo brother are the only two in there. I watch them for a while and sneer to myself at their pathetic little office and their pointless little lives. I think long and hard about throwing a brick through the window. I pick up a jagged lump of stone from the side-street opposite and test the weight of it in my hands. It'd do the job. Hopefully even hit one of those wankers and do some damage. I decide against it. It'd be a bit obvious it was me if it happened today. I'll wait until next week instead.

    I stop drinking and head home in an attempt to be a sober enough to get a hard-on when Alex arrives, but the three hours without drinking results in the early stages of a hang-over, so I crack open the first of the three bottles of wine I've bought for tonight just before she arrives. I'm disappointed as soon as I see her. She's pretty, with messy sandy hair and freckles but her arse is twice the size I was expecting. She's got huge tits under her top waiting to be unleashed but I suspect that's more because she's a bit fat rather than anything else. She's not in great nick. From the size of her I reckon she's been eating solidly since her profile pictures were taken. Still, she's here, so I fuck her anyway. Her belly and tits wobble around in time with my stroke. Half an hour in I wonder what the point of it is. She's enjoying it of course, but the alcohol has numbed my senses enough that I can barely be bothered to continue. She's just another shape beneath me at this point.

    I mechanically muster the enthusiasm for one final push to get over the finish line. I'm immediately disgusted by the presence of this sweaty, red blob of flesh next to me. I want her to leave. I tell her. She shouts. She cries. She goes. I don't feel good after Alex leaves. I open the window once she's gone to get the stale smell of sweat and fluids out. I stare at the ceiling for a bit and wonder how Amy's doing.

Chapter Thirty-nine

The hangover makes the normal Saturday gym sesh impossible. The thought of bench pressing and the treadmill makes me want to curl up and die. I text Gaz to let him know I won't be there. He doesn't reply. He's probably already in there, smashing out the sets. The bloke's a machine.

I head down to the local café for an emergency fry-up. I need some stodge inside of me, but the sloppy eggs make me want to puke. I push them to the edge of the plate and force down the sausage, bacon and beans. I half run home before they come back to haunt me. I'm not sure from which end. The fry-up hasn't helped so there's only one thing for it. Hair of the dog. I call Gaz again to see if he wants to hit the pub early but he doesn't answer. Must be putting in a hell of a session at the gym. I leave a message saying where I'll be. I pull on yesterday's clothes, which still have the lingering stench of yesterday all over them, and head down The Falcon again. They're still setting up the chairs and tables. Like me, the place reeks of last night's antics.

The same prick of a barman from yesterday makes me wait the two and a half minutes until twelve, eyeing me like I'm some sort of homeless drunk. I order a Stella and a Sambuca and sink them both by five-past. I grit my teeth and ignore the gurgling in my belly and pounding in my head as I wait for the alcohol to kick in and soothe the pain. I order another Stella, this time with a lemonade top to take the edge off. By the time I've half-finished it, my head clouds over and the agony become just a dull throb in the back of my skull. I set up in our usual spot in front of the big sports screen and try Gaz again to see when he'll be here. This time he picks up.

"Where have you been you big-eared bell-end," I say, "What time you getting here, I've got the normal seats and a beer with your name on it."

He stutters a bit. "Thing is mate, we're not going to be able to meet up today."

"What you talking about you big twat? Why not?"

"Um, well, me, Ben and Ritz are meeting Charlie down the pub later on. He told us what happened the other night. With you and his bird. He's bringing her down with him today to meet us."

He must be fucking joking. "You're going down the pub with that fucking grass Charlie, who stabbed me in the back and stole my eight grand, and his *fucking missus*?"

"Sorry mate," he says, "no hard feelings." He hangs up the phone before I can really get going about what a stupid bitch Alice is. Jesus fucking Christ. What the fuck is everyone playing at? I guess Marbella's off the table as well now. I do another Stella and follow it up with a Sambuca chaser. I head outside to the cash point. My bank balance isn't looking too clever.

I take twenty of my last ton out and head towards the Paddy Power. With no more wages coming after next week in I need a big result. I stick it on a six team accumulator; Liverpool, West Ham, Everton, Arsenal, Birmingham and Fulham. If that comes in it'll cover me for another couple of weeks while I sort another job out. It could actually end up being a nice bit of time off. Maybe I'll fuck off to Marbs on my own for the summer. I don't need those dickheads.

I pick up another four pack of Stella. I guess I'll be watching Soccer Saturday at home today then. On my tod. I sink another can while Paul Merson and Charlie Nicholas argue on the TV about whether Arsene Wenger should still be in charge at Arsenal. I couldn't give a shit as long as they win today. I'll always side with Merse though. Anyone who can win the Premier league while banging back that amount of booze and sniff is a legend in my book.

Chris comes back at half-time. He's been at some charity 10k run all day. Thinks he's Mo Farah or something. He plonks himself down on the other sofa and asks how my bets are getting on. Liverpool are two down at home which has pretty much sunk my bet. One of their useless African pricks has had a mare for both of the goals. I do another couple of cans while I watch the second half scores come in and my bet slip away. I have a quick look on the Autotrader website to check Audi TT prices. Eighty quid left in the bank and no cash coming in from Nick means I'm probably going to have to sell the beast to tide me over, which would be a real kick in the balls.

I ask Chris if he fancies a pizza and movie night tonight. I even dangle the carrot of Jurassic Park 4; Jurassic World, which is pretty much porn to him, but he's got plans with Ruby. Going out with her mates for one of their birthdays or something. Sad act. Gets a bird and immediately forgets who his mates are.

He's in and out within an hour, showered and changed with his glad rags on. Like a love-struck teenager who's seen his first pair of tits. It's embarrassing how much he chases around after her. I guess it's just me and the pizza tonight. I dig out a pair of old tracksuit bottoms and tee the film up while I use some of my remaining funds to order a pizza. Papa John's. Meat Feast. Stuffed Crust. Chris was right all along, there's an art to watching a film. Synchronising the arrival of your food with the start of the film is key. You can't have the food turn up half-way through. It ruins the momentum. It turns up about forty minutes later dropped off by some dour Somalian. I tell him to cheer up. Tell him at least he ain't working on a pirate ship. He doesn't get the joke though. Just takes the money and fucks off. Twenty five quid for a pizza and chicken wings. He's pretty much a fucking pirate in my book at those prices.

I press play and sink the rest of the beers. I laugh as various people are eaten by dinosaurs, some of which seem to have been made up for the purpose of the film. I move on to the last bottle of wine in the flat. The end of the film barely registers through the drunken haze. More dinosaurs, more people getting eaten, a few of the more famous actors manage to escape. Same as always. I try the lads again but no one picks up. I'm borderline comatose now, weighed down by a belly full of pizza and alcohol. I stumble into my room and clamber onto the bed. I can't even be bothered to turn out the light.

I wake around midnight. I'm lying on the bed fully clothed, still with my shoes on. There's an insistent tapping. I know what it is. I've been hearing it more and more recently. It's the slow rhythmic tapping against the wall of Chris's headboard. I hear Ruby as well. She's enjoying it. Really getting into it now. Not the timid little mouse she was when they first started shagging. I could barely hear her then, even when I held my ear to the wall. Now she's more vocal. More demanding. Sounds like she's quite a handful actually, the little minx. They're more comfortable together I guess. Like it used to be with Amy. Or Ellie even.

I wonder what the lads thought of Alice. She probably bored the shit out of them. Although she would have worn a low-cut top, so they probably loved her, the sad pricks. I wonder if they've hit Inferno's after the pub. That'll be shit without me. What they seem to be forgetting is the fact that it's my banter that holds the group together. They'll be realising that about now, probably all standing around at the bar trying to work out what to say to each other. They'll be leaving begging, drunk voicemails soon enough. As soon as they realise they're lost without me.

I look at my phone. No messages. No calls. Nothing.

Chapter Forty

It's been a year since all that shit with Charlie and the lads. Looking back, I don't blame him for what he did. I was out of line, I know that now. Still, eight grand is an expensive lesson. Occasionally I wonder what life would be like if he hadn't pocketed my cash. I'd still have the Audi, that's for sure. I had to sell it pretty soon after I left Barrie and Aberdeen. My bank account wasn't looking too clever and my mortgage payment on the flat was due. I ended up having to sell it cheap to make a quick sale. I loved that car. Still, all that's behind me now.

After the fall-out I didn't really hear much from the rest of the lads. I bumped into Ritz about two months back, which was fine. He's still a fat fucker. He was shovelling fish and chips into his mouth when I saw him. He'll be dead by forty-five if he carries on like that. I can see from Facebook and Instagram that the other boys haven't changed much either. Ben's still flogging his dodgy gear. Seems to be doing well judging by the size of his new gaff. I'm sure he's still shagging whatever he can get his hands on though. A leopard like that doesn't change its spots. Not like I have. Gaz is still just Gaz really. Down the gym everyday still. Big biceps and even bigger ears. I go to a different gym now that I've moved out of Clapham or I'm sure we'd meet up every now and again for a big sesh.

No, those boys will never change. They haven't got it in their locker. They all went to Marbella without me in the end. Invited Alice instead of me. On a lads' trip. Ridiculous. Bet it was well shit. Gaz, Ben, Ritz, Charlie and Alice. Just the thought of it makes me laugh.

I found out around the same time that Amy had gone and got engaged to that bloke who laid me out. That was a real kick up the arse. I realised how badly I'd fucked up. I couldn't carry on like I had been, so I decided to knuckle down and start taking dating seriously. Really concentrate on meeting someone decent. I met Sarah a few weeks later. She's the best thing that's ever happened to me.

I bumped into her in a bar in Waterloo. She works in a school round the corner and was out celebrating end of term with all the other teachers. I happened to be in there, meeting up with an old mate from back in the day. We got talking and the first thing that struck me was how nice she was. She seemed to really care about people. She was so passionate about the kids she teaches as well. Really wants them to succeed. She's decent and caring with a good heart. I knew straight away she was exactly the kind of girl I needed, especially after all that shit with Amy and the lads.

She's a bit different to the type I used to go for. She's not in to all that fake-tanning and bleaching her hair. She doesn't go out in anything too revealing and definitely doesn't post bikini-clad selfies of herself online. She's just not that kind of girl. She's got a really nice group of friends who get together every few months for a few drinks down the pub, but that's about it. Nothing too mental. They're all really normal, with long-term boyfriends. They seem alright. We talk a bit about football. One of the them supports Chelsea so we have a bit of banter. They're all coming over to ours tomorrow night for dinner. We're doing Come Dine With Me. Should be great fun.

Sarah and I went away at the end of the summer, so I still managed a bit of sunshine, despite missing out on the lads' trip. She wasn't sure at first, as we'd only been together a couple of months at that point. She came round in the end though. It was lovely. Completely different to any holiday I'd ever been on. Proper relaxing it was. Just me and Sarah and a little bed and breakfast in the south of France. Banging food and decent wine. We did a load of walks on the beach, ate croissants for breakfast and drank local wine, that kind of stuff. Not like the KFC, cheap vodka and groping people in foam parties those losers would have got up to in Marbella. We got really comfortable together on that holiday. We really began to understand each other.

We're having our standard Thursday night tonight, watching a few episodes of Lost. We're halfway through season three at the moment, getting through a couple of episodes a night. I enjoyed the first series, with monsters and polar bears and all that running about, but truth be told it's boring me to tears now. She likes it though so I don't say anything. The last time I spent time doing this sort of thing was about a year ago, with Amy. Sarah leans into me. I put my arm round her and kiss her on the top of the forehead. She smiles up at me. I smile back. She's a good girl Sarah, really looks after me. I give her another kiss on the forehead and ask if she wants to watch another one, despite the fact I've got no idea what's going on with the storyline. Most of the last few episodes have just been people sitting in cages.

Sarah checks her watch. "We'd better not," she says, "it's nearly half-nine." She's got a point. We like to be in bed by ten ideally on a weeknight, to make sure we get our full eight hours in. She gets up at six-fifteen every morning as she starts work at seven. I never realised how hard teachers work. Always thought it was practically part-time. It took a hell of a lot of getting used to, her alarm going off that early, especially as I don't need to be up until eight. Back in the day I would have stopped seeing a girl for a lot less than that. Especially if they insisted on drying their hair in the bedroom every morning like she does, stopping me going back to sleep. But relationships are about compromise, so I don't say anything.

She heads upstairs first to start getting ready for bed and leaves me watching Sky Sports News. Sarah's not a fan of football so this time before bed is about the only chance I get to watch it in the house. Back in the day I watched every match I could find on TV.

Any night, any league, I watched it. I even got into the Australian League for a bit, even though it was shite. But things are different now. You have to compromise. I head up at five to ten to clean my teeth and slip on my pyjama bottoms, which were a Christmas gift from her grandmother.

Sarah's already in bed. I look at her, doing her deep-breathing exercises. She can't see me as she's already got her eye-mask on. She's got her retainer in as well. She's a bit obsessive about her teeth. It makes her snore a bit, which took a bit of getting used to, but you have to compromise if you want a relationship to work. I slide under the covers as gently as possible. I can tell she's already asleep so I don't want to wake her. Although she's got her earplugs in so there's not much chance of that. I stare at the ceiling as my eyes adjust to the darkness. I clear my mind as much as possible. I remove any thoughts of the lads, the Audi, Charlie and my money. Thoughts like that are for the old me. I'm different now.

Chapter Forty-one

The offices of Russell and Marrs are pretty much the same as every other estate agency in the world. A little shopfront on the high street, a few desks and a steady stream of idiots through the door. It's quieter than Barrie and Aberdeen used to be, as it's in New Malden, a sleepy little town a couple of miles outside Kingston upon Thames, a far cry from the relative metropolis of Clapham High Street, but the days are pretty much the same.

I'm stuck on the lettings desk over here, which is a bit of a comedown considering I was the top sales guy at Barrie and Aberdeen, before Charlie stitched me up and David stuck the knife in, but beggars can't be choosers and I try not to think about the past too much. Things are different now.

Russell and Marrs is owned by a couple of guys, both called John. We only see one of them most of the time. John Marrs manages the day to day. Nice bloke. Nicer than David turned out to be anyway, albeit a bit dim. He didn't ask too many questions when I applied for the job, which was ideal. He practically cracked a boner when he saw the level of my sales experience. I left out the bit about getting fired. Luckily he never checked. His business partner, the other John, comes in once a week to check up on everything. He's clearly the brains of the operation.

There's me and an old woman called Julie on the lettings side. She's been here years. Works part-time. She's rotund to say the least. She spends half the day banging on about losing weight, and the other half shoving cakes down her neck. She doesn't mind doing Saturdays though, which is a touch as I only have to do one a month. I'm pretty sure she does it just to get away from her husband whose various short-comings are the other things she relentlessly yaks on about.

There's a couple of young lads on the sales desks. Matt and Jamie. They remind me of me, before I changed. Always going on about women, going out, having a laugh. They've got great banter. We're having our customary Friday pub lunch today down the Railway. It's a bit of a dive but the burgers are half-decent. The rest of the sales desk is made up of Gerry, who wears an Italian designer suit despite being an estate agent. He's a bit of a cock. Then there's Lucy. Pushing forty but still decent. In the old days I would have slung one up her a couple of times. Not now though, I've changed.

I've got a viewing to rush through before lunch. A four bedroom detached for a Korean family. I show her round but she's got absolutely no idea what I'm talking about. Doesn't speak a word of English. She nods a lot and babbles at me, so I presume she's keen. Her husband's employers are picking up the rental tab so I don't suppose it matters too much. We get a lot of them round here. Highest concentration of Korean's outside of Korea apparently. No idea why.

Matt and Jamie are already in the pub when I get back, so I dump my keys on my desk and head over. They've got a pint waiting for me. I can taste the vodka they've spiked it with on the first sip. They must think I was born yesterday. I wait and swap pints with Jamie when he's not looking. He takes a gulp and doesn't notice. Amateur.

"You coming out with us tomorrow night?" asks Matt. "We're hitting The Grand in Clapham. Should be loads of fanny in there."

"Can't lads, sorry." I say, "We've got Sarah's friends coming over to the flat tomorrow night. We're doing Come Dine With Me."

They both look at me like I've got three heads. We had a quality night out together a few months back, on the Russell and Marrs Christmas do. We were downing Sambucas and pinching arses all over The Clapham Grand like it was our last day on earth. Just like I used to do with Charlie and the lads back in the day. These two saw a side of me I'd tried to keep under wraps since I moved out here. They've been trying to get me to go out with them ever since. It's be good banter but it's not worth the grief I'd get from Sarah. I got a right row after the Christmas do.

"A few beers after work tonight then?" asks Jamie. He already knows what my answer will be. I try not to go for beers with these two. We'd have a laugh but it's easier to say no to the first pint than the fourth. Or the seventh. Besides, tonight's date night with Sarah.

"Sorry lads," I say. I don't need to give them any more than that. They know I'd love to. It's just not really possible these days.

I only have the one pint at lunch with them. Carling, as I can't handle Stella anymore. I'd better not have another or I'll reek of it. Sarah will sniff that out in a flash. Not worth the hassle. I don't want her thinking I'm slipping back into my old ways. Not that she knows the half of it. Matt needs some advice on a girl he's trying to pull. I patiently explain to him about picking a first date bar close to his place, just in case. Then somewhere decent for dinner on the second date, if she's worth it. He shows me a picture. She's tidy. Definitely worth it. Then for the final nudge over the line he needs to invite her over for dinner. If she doesn't put out by that point she's not worth the effort.

I'm kind of a Buddha figure to the lads. They come to me for advice on anything like this. A bit like Gaz and Ritz used to do. We finish up and head back to the office. It's been a good week so John breaks out the crisps and fizzy drinks at four o'clock. That cock David would never have done something like this. It's that kind of thing that makes this place a much more relaxed place to work. No one needlessly going through your work all the time, banging on about process and no one stabbing you in the back to get their hands on your bonus money. It's different at Russell and Marrs.

John closes the office door early and we sit in a circle and chat about what we've got planned for the weekend. John's going to be in the garden, continuing his meagre efforts at a vegetable patch. He brought in his first batch of carrots last week. They were tiny. Probably about the size of Charlie's cock. Julie's doing a cake sale tomorrow for a kid's charity. No doubt she'll have to donate half her salary by the time she's finished. Matt and Jamie are obviously pretty pumped up about their night out in Clapham, much to everyone else's amusement. I've no doubt they'll have some stories for me on Monday morning. Lucy's got a date Saturday night. She's always going on dates and then blurting out the miserable details to us when she's had a couple of drinks. Normally while she's crying her eyes out. A year or so ago I'd definitely have given her one a couple of times, just to keep her morale up, but I'm different now so I keep my distance.

Gerry's going to some exclusive restaurant opening in Mayfair, but he's a cock so everyone tunes out while he's talking. John even asks me what I've got planned while Gerry's still speaking, which pisses him right off. I tell them about Come Dine With Me. Jamie tries to take the piss but Julie think it's the most exciting thing she's ever heard so his banter gets drowned out. Lucy sticks up for me. She wants to be invited to the next one. When she's met the right guy. Which means it will never happen.

"Sure I can't tempt you for a quick beer?" asks Matt as we're tidying the office chairs away at five. I'm sorely tempted but I stick to my guns. I can't miss date night with Sarah.

Chapter Forty-two

Sarah doesn't like Nando's so we go for Pizza Express on our Friday date nights. I get the American, she gets the Sloppy Giuseppe and we share a portion of garlic dough balls. We always take it away so that we can eat it in front of the TV and a couple of episodes of Lost. The bald guy, the Arab and the fit one are fighting with some one-eyed Russian who lives on some kind of farm. I've got absolutely no idea what's going on. Sarah loves it though so I don't say anything. You've got to make compromises in a relationship.

Sarah's had this little house in New Malden for about five years. It's a pretty little two up two down with a decent garden. I moved in with her about six months ago. We'd only been dating about four months but it just felt right. Also, I was really struggling with money, so it made sense from that point of view. Her mortgage is tiny. I ended up moving out of my flat when Chris and Ruby started making noises about moving in together. It made more financial sense for me to leave and let them rent the whole place from me. I did them a bit of a deal, which covers my mortgage with enough left over to give Sarah some. Taking everything into account I'm a few hundred quid better off now than before, which is a result.

I've been over and visited them a few times since I moved out. Ruby's really made the place nice. Much nicer than when I was around anyway. Me and Sarah have met up with them for dinner a couple of times as well, but it was a bit awkward. Chris knows about my past, some of it anyway, and I don't want him putting his foot in it in front of Sarah. Also, Ruby saw me during the aftermath of the fall out with Charlie and the lads and it wasn't pretty. I wasn't in a good place. Sarah and her seemed to get on well so I put a stop to that. Didn't want them getting too chummy and her mentioning some of the rotters she saw coming out of my room during those couple of months.

We get through three episodes tonight and most of a bottle of Pinot. Sarah likes a glass most nights. It helps her unwind after a hard day at school, but on date night she lets her hair down a bit more. Sometimes we end up getting through nearly two bottles. We don't start a fourth episode of Lost tonight or we'll miss Alan Carr. He's Sarah's favourite comedian. I prefer something a bit more edgy, like Frankie Boyle, but Sarah says he's too offensive and his jokes are too 'base', whatever that means.

On Fridays I get myself ready for bed first. It's all part of our ritual. I clean my teeth and put on a pair of my better boxer shorts. Sarah emerges from the bathroom about fifteen minutes later wearing her standard seductive ensemble; a lacy vest top, in black, coupled with lacy black French knickers. Sarah's tall and skinny, with not much arse to speak of, so the French knickers don't stretch across her arse-cheeks like I've seen on some girls, but they're French knickers, so they look hot anyway. The black lace really contrasts nicely against her pale skin. She always makes an effort on date night.

She slides under the covers and we begin our usual routine. I do most of the work, Sarah's old fashioned like that, but I don't mind. Date night only comes round once a week so I'm hardly likely to complain. Sometimes the weeks seem to crawl by, waiting for it, but this one's gone quickly; it feels like only yesterday Sarah was sliding herself in beside me wearing those French knickers. Tonight the wine seems to have had an effect and she's feeling a little more adventurous than she has done for a while. We cycle through three positions before her customary whimpering lets me know I've done a satisfactory job. She tidies her hastily discarded black lace and pulls on her pyjamas. Date Night is officially over.

I head to the bathroom and find her already snoring slightly by the time I return. It's not quite what I was used to with Amy, or Ellie, or most of the others thinking about it, but things are different now. It's been ten months, six of them living together, and we're a bit past the whole *ripping our clothes off* stage. It's nice. I never got passed that initial relentless shagging part with anyone, where you can't keep your hands off each other and all you think about is getting back into bed. I never realised how rewarding it is to settle down with someone and not to have to think about sex all the time. Not that I've stopped thinking about it, obviously, I just don't act upon it every moment of the day. Now we do things like talk, watch Alan Carr and read the Sunday papers together over brunch. It's satisfying on a much deeper level. Charlie used to joke that I didn't have a deeper level. I guess the joke's on him, the back-stabbing prick.

Thinking about the old days stirs more than memories inside me. I nuzzle up to Sarah and kiss her neck gently, while rubbing my foot against hers, to see if there's any chance of another round. She pushes me away. Sarah never appreciates being woken up. She does work bloody hard though so it's not surprising she's so tired all the time. Besides, we've got a late one tomorrow doing Come Dine With Me so it's best we get some rest.

I'm not quite ready for sleep yet. It's only eleven so I turn on the bedside lamp and read a few chapters of Gazza's autobiography. Some of the banter he got up to in the early years was classic. Sarah's been trying to get me to read more, she even bought me Bravo Two Zero for Christmas, but I found it a bit heavy going. She turned her nose up a bit when I started reading football autobiographies. She said they were all morons with more money than brain cells but she's always watching some bollocks about Kim Kardashian, so I don't know why that's any different. I much prefer reading about Gazza and all the laughs he had with the lads back in the day. Mind you, if he'd changed, like I have, he probably wouldn't be in the state he is now. As Sarah always says to me, everyone's got to grow up sometime.

Chapter Forty-three

Sarah's friend Dawn is the first to arrive, with her boyfriend Tim. Dawn works at school with Sarah, teaching one of the other junior classes. We do that double cheek kissing thing people do when they're trying to be sophisticated. Tim and I shake hands. I'm gutted they're here first as Tim's got zero banter and Dawn's one of those girls that finds stuff that isn't funny hilarious. She's not attractive in any way and has absolutely no redeeming features. She's already beyond fat and well on the way to being obese. Sarah would never admit it, but I'm pretty sure Dawn is the reason she bought an extra pound of mince for tonight's chilli. Our evening is Mexican-themed so Sarah doles out a pair of Sombreros to them as soon as they get through the door. Dawn practically pisses herself laughing.

Emily and Luke are the next to arrive thank fuck. Emily went to the same college as Sarah. She's quite a hard-drinker and works up in the city. I get the impression she put it about a bit before she met Luke, who's a real east-end boy. He used to be a trader up in town until the economy went tits up. He's been off work for a couple of months now but Emily earns a fair wedge, so he doesn't seem to be in too much hurry to find himself a new job. They've got a luxury pad on the river somewhere near Greenwich. Getting over to them for their round of Come Dine With Me is going to be a real ball-ache. Sarah hands out their sombreros. Luke and I look at each other but don't say anything. We both know we look like a right pair of knob-heads. I leave him in the living room to make small talk with Tim while I go to the front door to let in the final couple; Rob and Beth.

What Beth is doing working in a school I will never know, other than giving young boys confusing feelings they aren't old enough to understand. By rights she should be on the cover of Sport Illustrated.

Or at the very least modelling in a couple of catalogues. In the glory days of Loaded and FHM she'd definitely have been made a few offers, but instead she spends her days teaching kids how to colour between the lines. Rob is some sort of I.T geek. How he managed to snare her is one of life's great mysteries. To his credit he knows full well Beth is out of his league, which is why he proposed to her a couple of years ago. Locked her in. Smart move. He needs to get her down the aisle soon, or at least stick a kid in her or someone else will nip in there. Someone more on her level.

Sarah's watching like a hawk so I greet them as if it hasn't occurred to me that Beth's an absolute belter. Sarah's got a bit of a complex about her. She's always bringing it up, ever since she first introduced me to her a couple of months ago. I've always managed to dodge the accusations by saying she's a bit fake-looking for me, with her blonde hair, fake tan and massive jugs. Not my type at all. But I'm only ever one misplaced look or lingering stare away from the doghouse so I make a big fuss of Rob, ask him how work is, even though I have no real idea what he does. I give Beth a cursory peck on the cheek, despite the ridiculously low-cut top and short skirt combo she's wearing. I don't look at her perfectly tanned and toned legs at all and I barely notice her tits press against my chest when she leans in to kiss me hello. I give them their sombreros and beckon them into the dining room.

Sarah's put on some playlist she downloaded earlier, some weird Mexican music, and passes round the sangria. We make small talk, trying to ignore the fact we're standing around in giant sombreros and having to shout over what sounds like a constant loop of the Doritos advert.

Sarah scurries around in the kitchen for five minutes before telling us all to take our seats for the first course; nachos. She points out everything on the table, all the salsas, cheeses and sour cream. She glares at me as she points out her home made guacamole, which was the source of a tense conversation earlier in the day. She didn't appreciate it when I pointed out that the two avocados she bought from Waitrose specifically to make it, cost four times the price of a pot of already-made guacamole. And that's before she even factored in the time it took her to make the bloody stuff. She told me to piss off. I don't mention it to anyone, despite the fact I know the blokes would all be on my side. We all race against time to taste the nachos before Dawn hoovers up the lot.

In between courses, Sarah's organised some entertainment, in an attempt to make sure we score as highly as possible in the Come Dine With Me stakes. She dashes out of the room for a quick costume change before returning to do a passable impression of a flamenco dance. I accompany her on maracas but realise approximately two seconds in that I have not drunk nearly enough sangria to be doing this.

The girls get into it. Tim claps along slightly out of time. Luke and Rob try not to laugh in my face. A year or so ago I would have thought the whole thing was tragic, but you have to do this kind of thing when you're in a relationship. Mercifully, Sarah dances for only one song. I slug back a glass of Sangria as Sarah brings out the main course. A mountain of chilli. This is my contribution to the evening. I'm no Gordon Ramsey but I do make a mean chilli. My secret ingredient is sweetcorn. It sweetens the whole thing right up. I've made an absolute truckload and everyone goes to town on it. I'm in the charge of the next round of entertainment once the chilli's been cleared away. Sarah scowls as I slap a bottle of Tequila down on the table and make everyone do two shots each. It's not quite in keeping with Sarah's aim for a sophisticated evening, but everyone loves it.

We have some kind of flan for dessert. No idea what it's all about but it's decent. We fire our way through the remainder of the Tequila when we're done and crank up the Doritos music. The girls are dancing round their sombreros while the lads are having a bit of banter. It's turned into a bit of a party. Dawn's knackered after a couple of minutes and has to sit down. She's developed sweat patches in some unfortunate areas.

Beth grabs my hand a couple of times and tries to get me to dance. I can feel Sarah's eyes boring a hole into the side of my head so I decline. The night peters out after an hour or so, mainly because we're out of booze. I told Sarah we needed more drink but she wouldn't have it. She couldn't see how six of us were going to get through six bottles of red but now the parties over and it's only just gone ten. I can't help but feel it'll cost us when the scores are handed out. Dawn and Tim are the last to leave. She mine-sweeps the last piece of flan on her way out.

There's a shedload of tidying up to do, but in a break with normal tradition, Sarah wants to leave it for the morning. She doesn't even put the dishes into soak. We're in bed by eleven. Lights out. "Tonight went well I think," I offer into the darkness.

She's quiet for a few moments before responding. "You fancy Beth don't you?"

Jesus Christ, not this shit again. She's always going on about Beth. Every time we see her. Certainly her face is great and she's got an incredible body. And yes, she's got fantastic eyes and beautifully toned legs. As well as one hell of an arse. Those things would all have appealed to me back when I was only interested in superficial things. But I'm different now. I'm looking for more than that. I almost wish we hadn't invited her over now. Almost. "Don't be ridiculous." I say. "You're the only one for me."

"I just think you'd prefer to be with someone like her."

"Maybe back in the old days." I concede. "Back when I was an idiot. When all I did was drink and go out. Before I realised there was more to relationships. Before I took the time to understand someone properly. But I'm different now. I want someone I truly connect with. Someone I love. Someone like you."

It occurs to us both that this is the first time that I've told Sarah I love her.

She tells me she loves me too. At least she's stopped banging on about Beth.

Chapter Forty-four

Sarah gives my hand a little squeeze as we sit down at her aunt's dinner table. One of her cousins is piling a vast amount of roast beef onto my plate while her dad's dumping an army's worth of roast potatoes alongside. The wine's flowing but I stick to diet coke. I haven't drunk Tequila for a long time and my guts aren't thanking me for last night.

Sarah knows I never really did any of this family stuff before we got together, so she fusses over me like I'm a child in her class at school. She needn't bother, we've been coming here most Sundays for about six months now. It took her a while to convince me to come along, but once I'd moved in with her I couldn't really put it off any more. Her family have really taken to me as well. I go to Chelsea sometimes with her Dad and Uncle. They're season ticket holders. I have to keep my head down a bit when we do go, in case I bump into some of the lads from the old days, back when we used to scrap with the oppo's mob every week, but Sarah's family sit in the posh end so there's not much chance of that. We're not down The Bridge today because of the family lunch, but the game starts at four, so we'll watch it afterwards on their eighty-inch screen. It's pretty much like being there when you've got a TV that big.

Her cousins are decent too. The older one, Kate, is quite fit. She wears these little tight jeans that would have driven the old me crazy. Sometimes I see her looking at me, but I keep my distance. Things are different now. I'm different. I squeeze her a bit tighter than the rest of them when I'm saying goodbye, but that's as far as it goes.

All this took a fair bit of getting used to, sitting with a load of grown-ups every weekend. Some of the stuff they talk about makes my head hurt. Politics and something called the *footsie*. They're always talking about some article they've read in the economist or the Observer. I only ever read The Sun, and even then it's only for the football. I can join in a bit when they talk about property though. I'm only in lettings these days but I know what's going on out there. What Sarah's made me realise is that this is what life's about. Spending time with someone you care about and weekends with the family. Not crazy nights out and non-stop shagging.

After the aunts have finished fattening us all up we head into the TV room and take up our usual seats. Her dad and uncle have their own armchairs on either side of a big leather sofa. I sit alongside Jason, another of Sarah's cousins, who's also a season ticket holder down The Bridge. I find watching the game with Sarah's family awkward. I'm constantly forcing swearwords and abuse back down my throat to make sure I don't shatter the respectable image I've managed to convince them is the real me. It's particularly difficult today as Chelsea throw two early goals away to Arsenal and practically give up before half time. No passion for the shirt at all. I suppress a final outburst, likely involving the words *prick*, *wanker* or worse when we concede a third with five minutes to go.

"Ah well," says Sarah's Uncle. "More wine?"

"I'm ok thanks," I say. A year ago I'd be looking for a fight after a result like that. Now I'm turning down a glass of Rosé.

We say our goodbyes and hit the road. Sarah's family live in North London, an hour or so around the M25. On a good day. Today is not a good day. The traffic is murder. I do my best not to hurl abuse at the various muppets blocking the road. The gridlock clears within a couple of junctions though, before I lose my rag too much. I reckon I could have done this in under an hour back in the day, when I had the Audi. I can't really throw our ten-year old Civic around like that, so I sit in the middle lane doing seventy. One of the things I like about being with Sarah is the comfortable silence. No banter, no messing about, just peace and quiet all the way home. We don't need to say anything to be happy in each other's company. It's a bit different to the constant banter and activity of the old days but I like it. I remember one trip to Brighton when we didn't say a single word to each other. We just listened to Coldplay's new album the entire way down there. It was lovely.

We get back around seven-thirty. Sarah's keen to squeeze in another episode or two of Lost. We'll have to crack on with it pretty quickly as we normally like to be in bed by nine-thirty on a Sunday night. She always says you can't get the Sunday night fear if you're already asleep, which makes sense I suppose. Not that I really get the fear. Working in lettings at Russell and Marrs is a piece of piss. It's not like the stress I used to get in sales. All the wheeling and dealing, negotiating and bartering. It used to be fun but I like the quieter life now. The most excitement I get now is squeezing as much money as possible out of student's deposits. I'm a genius at it. John should really be giving me some sort of commission.

Sarah's life is a bit more stressful. I wouldn't be able to handle thirty-odd six year olds running about, pissing and shitting themselves all day. Especially when half of them are Korean and don't speak a word of English. I bet they're shit-hot at maths though. They always are. Apparently there's something called an Ofsted inspection coming up, which has got all the teachers shitting it. It sounds like a right ball-ache.

Sarah's got her eye-mask on and retainer in and I can tell she's getting antsy about me taking my time getting ready for bed, so I get my arse into gear and into the bathroom. I'm in bed just before the nine-thirty but Sarah still makes a point of checking the time as if I'm late. Christ, the lads would never believe I go to bed at this time on a Sunday night these days, if they could see it. She turns off the light and is out for the count pretty sharpish. I guess that's the advantage of an eye-mask and ear plugs. The truth is, I struggle to sleep this early. Back in the day I rarely went to bed before midnight, and if I did it was because I had someone in bed with me, which meant there was no chance we'd be asleep until at least two. Lying here in the dark feels like a couple of wasted hours really. I could be watching Match of The Day 2, not that I want to after today's shit-show. I could even watch another box-set. Anything instead of bloody episode of Lost but it's not worth the earache if I wake Sarah up, so I close my eyes and try to clear my mind enough to drift off.

Chapter Forty-five

My old insomnia's started to creep back in over the last few months. What sleep I do get is restless and sporadic and by the time Sarah's alarm goes off in the morning I feel like I've not been to bed at all. Like most nights, I'm lying in the pitch black, zoning out and staring at the ceiling with a million thoughts firing around my brain, when a low buzzing sound focuses my attention. My eyes dart towards the low level glow of my phone as the screen pierces through the darkness. I glance over at Sarah but she's still dead to the world, her chest rising and falling evenly, her sleep guarded by her eye-mask and earplugs. I slowly slide my hand down to the side of the bed as smoothly as possibly, desperate not to disturb Sarah's unconscious state. I gradually manoeuvre my hand down to where my phone sits, on the pile of dirty clothes I'd taken off when I got into bed. I roll onto my side and unlock my phone, keeping it under the level of the mattress, still out of sight, just in case Sarah stirs. I throw another look her way. She's still out. The source of the disturbance is a new message. As soon as I heard it buzz I knew who it was from. A smile creeps across my face as I realise I'm right. I glance at the time on my phone as I open the message; it's just before one.

I want to see you, it says.

I knew this was coming. I could feel it heading this way from the first time we saw each other. I saw the spark in her eyes the night we were introduced in the pub. She sent me a friendly Facebook message a couple of days later, just to open the lines of communication. Our chats became more regular over time, with an increasingly flirty undercurrent. At some point we made an excuse to move our weekly Facebook messages to texts. They quickly became daily conversations. Every now and again there's a drunken phone call, when one of us is pissed enough to forget the risks. All of it done in secret. All of it done behind people's backs. It's been heading for something like this since the outset.

The stirring is immediate, both in my mind and my boxers. I imagine her lying next to me. Completely naked, that body of hers pressing against me. I imagine what we'd do to each other, like I've imagined so many times before. The fact I know she's thinking the same thing is exhilarating. I glance over at Sarah. She's still dead to the world, her nose whistling slightly when she exhales, her breathing totally undisturbed, none-the-wiser to the mental quandary I'm wrestling with alongside her. I slip silently out from under the covers and pad down the hallway and into the bathroom, clutching my phone. I gently close the door behind me and click the lock shut as silently as I can.

I re-read the message. I want to see her too. More than anything, but I've changed enough over the last year to know it's wrong. We'd be stepping over the line. Flirting via text message and the odd drunken phone call is one thing but if we meet up we both know it'd go further. We wouldn't be able to control ourselves. There'd be no turning back. I think of Sarah. Of our nights curled up on the sofa and our cosy life together in her house. I think of date nights on Fridays and watching Chelsea with her family. I think of how hurt she'd be if she ever found out I was even speaking to someone like this. I'd be risking everything. I tap out a reply.

We can't.

I want to feel relief as I send it but all I feel is regret. A sad disappointment that I have to deny myself the one thing I want the most.

She goes quiet for a few minutes before replying.

This is so hard, she says.

She's right. It's torture. We both know how much we want each other. I run the cold tap for a while and stare at myself hard in the mirror. I splash the water on my face, stare harder.

I want to see you too, I reply. I know, even as I type it, it's wrong but I can't stop myself. The thought of her wanting me makes me makes feel alive. Just like I used to feel when I used to walk into a bar and see all the girls looking at me, knowing I could have whoever I wanted. A rogue thought appears; maybe we should. Just once. Just to get it out of our systems. Maybe we just need to release the tension so that we can move on.

When can we meet? She says.

Crunch time.

How much have I really changed? I look at the message and imagine us together. I know how good it'd be. I know it'd be everything I've been missing out on the last year. It'd be all the urgent intensity that's painfully absent from the Friday night routine with Sarah. But I can't risk everything I've built with her. I don't want to risk hurting her after everything she's done for me.

I can't.

I type it out. Send it. Turn my phone off. I know I should feel proud that I've passed the test but I don't. I just feel gutted.

Sarah stirs as I slide back under the covers.

"Everything ok sweetheart?" She asks, in that slightly garbled speech that people use when they're half asleep. And wearing a retainer. She reaches out to me blindly, her eye-mask doing its job. I take her hand in mine. Through the darkness I can just make out the patches of toothpaste she's smeared over patches of her face to dry out her skin.

"Go back to sleep." I whisper to her. She doesn't need a second invitation and rolls over, grunting her agreement.

I stare at the ceiling through the gloom and listen to the rhythmic sound of the air whistling through Sarah's nose. I wrestle with my decision for a while, even though I know it's the right one.

Things are different now, I tell myself. I'm different now.

Chapter Forty-six

"Working late tonight?" asks John. He's right to be surprised; this is the first time I've been in the office after five o'clock since I started working at Russell and Marrs.

"I've got a viewing at six-thirty over at those new show homes on Kingston Road," I say.

He looks confused. Which isn't that unusual, but in this case it's for a reason. "I didn't think we'd been given the go ahead by the developer yet?" He's spot on. Very occasionally he surprises me by being vaguely aware of what's going on in his own office.

"One of them called earlier, while you were out at lunch," I say, thinking quickly on my feet. "They're not completely ready yet, but the bloke asked me to do this viewing for him tonight as a favour."

John buys it, tells me not to stay too late. He doesn't want me to keep Sarah waiting too long by working too hard. He heads out the door whistling. He's a lovely guy, just a bit dim. The perfect boss if you ever want to do anything on the sly.

I head over to the show home for quarter-past six. I park up round the corner and walk the couple of hundred metres to the empty house, checking around every few metres to see if anyone's clocked me, but it's unnecessary; the workmen are long since gone, all clocked off on the dot of five, and the sun's already disappearing behind the rest of the semi-finished new builds. The clocks go forward next week, but for now, I use the early darkness to my advantage and creep up to the house unseen. I managed to nab the front door key from John's desk drawer while he was out earlier, and it opens up the lock with a satisfying clunk. I take my shoes off as soon as I step inside. I can't afford anyone to know I've been here.

It'd be just my luck to walk a trail of dog-shit all over the fresh carpet and get rumbled.

These show homes give me the creeps. Everything's so perfect. Gleaming windows with freshly painted window sills. Pristine furniture, some it still wrapped, sitting on top of spanking new carpets. The whole place is freshly decorated, yet to be ruined by anyone living in it. There's a vase of flowers sitting on the dining table, but like everything else here it's superficial and fake. The petals are plastic and lifeless when you get close enough to touch. Everything about the place is too perfect.

I walk upstairs, through to the bedroom at the back. I hang my suit jacket on the back of the door. It's safe to put the light on back here, away from the prying eyes of the main road so I turn on the bedside lamp, which gives the place an eerie glow. I sit on the edge of the bed, on the fresh and unruffled grey duvet set. It feels like I'm sitting in a hotel room.

I hear a knock on the front door. A light and uncertain tapping. Unsure if this is the right place. I pad through the dark hallway towards the front door. I open it and immediately realise why I'm here. Why all of this was so inevitable. Why I stayed up all night regretting saying no to her and why this morning I changed my mind.

"Hi Beth," I say.

"Hi Danny," she purrs. We look at each other for a moment. It's tense, exciting.

"You're not going to leave a lady standing out on the doorstep are you?" She says.

I glance around behind her, to check we're alone, to check no one's seen us, before I beckon her in and she steps inside to join me in the shadows. She's wearing a long grey coat. She opens it and it slides to the living room floor, leaving her standing there in just her red high heels and matching lingerie. I drink her in. Those eyes, that skin, that body. It's everything I imagined it would be.

"Maybe you can show me the bedroom first," she says.

We don't even make it that far.

I make it home by nine. Sarah's a bit arsey with me as she wanted to get through three episodes of Lost tonight to finish off the series. My late night appointment at the show home put paid to that. Maybe we'll get through two if we're lucky.

"Sorry," I say as I sit down beside her, "the viewing went on for ages."

She doesn't say anything, just grunts in my direction and presses play on the remote. I kiss her on the forehead as she nestles into her normal position on my shoulder.

"You smell nice," she murmurs, obviously taking in the lightly scented soap I used to scrub off this evening's evidence; the smell of Beth's perfume and the lingering hum of nearly two hours of frantic, intense shagging. Thankfully the show homes power shower was fully-fitted and working. I'll be sure to mention how good it is when we finally get the go ahead from the developer to do real viewings.

We get through a couple of episodes of Lost. It bores me to tears now but tonight I barely notice. I've got other things on my mind. Sarah heads off to get ready for bed just after ten. She's already got her retainer in and eye-mask on by the time I head into the bathroom to clean my teeth. I turn on the tap and take my phone out from my pocket. Beth's already been in touch:

Tonight was amazing. When can we meet up again?

I stare at myself in the mirror as the sink fills up in front of me. I don't need to think about how to respond. I've been turning it over in my mind ever since I got home. I weighed it up as Sarah's head lay against my shoulder. While images of what I'd been doing only a couple of hours earlier ran on a continuous loop through my head. Everything's clear to me now; it was all just one big blip. I just needed to be reminded. I know what's important to me now. I know what I need to do.

I type out my response:

How about tomorrow?

Acknowledgements

To the best influence a boy could ever have, Charles Hutton. You once said you believed I'd go on to do something great. Even if I never do, the fact you said it will forever urge me on. I wish you could be here to see me try.

My mum, the single greatest woman to ever walk the earth.

Georgia, for literally everything, particularly putting up with me disappearing for hours on end to scribble in notebooks.

To my Auntie Marie – probably my biggest fan! Sorry about all the swearing in this one…

John Marrs, your constant support has really pushed me forward with this. Danny wouldn't be the man he turned out to be if it wasn't for your encouragement. Thanks for having such belief in my little stories, I am eternally grateful.

Kath Middleton, the sharpest eyes in the west. Thanks so much for your proofreading skills, I am forever grateful, and thanks for all the fabulous book recommendations. I apologise profusely for all the puppies harmed in the making of this book.

Tracy Fenton, fairy godmother to so many authors out there, and the indefatigable force behind The Book Club on Facebook. Thank you for your eagle eyes, your kind words, your support and your advice.

To the genius Mike Thomas, your kind words of encouragement, from way back when I was tinkering around with short stories about tenants, have been a huge boost to my confidence. Quite how you aren't a millionaire author yet I'll never know. It's surely only around the corner.

Nick Bond, my A-level English teacher. I suspect I would have been the longest odds in the class back then to be the one ending up doing this – your advice and encouragement over the last few years has been gratefully received.

Ralph Welch – a real talent and a proper gent. Looking forward to reading the adventures of Mr Cash. Have faith, it's going to fly.

Ian Ayris, for John Sissons, the foul-mouthed narrator I was looking for.

The authors and readers of The Book Club on Facebook (it really is **THE** book club) for the relentlessly fantastic book recommendations and support for authors. It really does make it all worthwhile to see the passion people have for books of all types.

Spiffing Covers for a stupendous cover – I love it, you absolutely nailed it.

The staff of Gordon Bennett in Surbiton, particularly Agnes, Farhia and Josie for keeping the random bloke full of tea and coffee while he scribbled his way through six notebooks in four months.

Last, but by no means least, every single person who takes the time to buy and read this. Having someone read something I made up in my head is the greatest of pleasures.

Also by Andrew Webber

How would you live today, if you knew there was no tomorrow?

Follow the lives of three ordinary people as one tragic day unfolds that changes everything;

Country girl Laura, struggling to cope with her move to London. Frugal John, desperately saving to get on the property ladder and womaniser Charlie, racing through as many conquests as he can.

Today is a story of the struggles of modern life, society's obsession with planning for the future and the lack of control we have over the hand fate deals us.

TODAY

ANDREW WEBBER

"Today is a cracking tale of contemporary life in the unforgiving city that is modern day London. Both disturbing and thought-provoking in equal measure." – Ian Ayris, author of Abide with Me & April Skies.

"Really taps into the melancholy of modern times" – Sid Lambert, author of Cashing In.

ABOUT THE AUTHOR

Andrew Webber lives in London, England. During the week he works in the advertising industry, but spends the weekends scribbling in notebooks and writing character-based stories, few of which make it far enough to be typed up. Occasionally one makes its way into the public domain.

He can be found on twitter (@mrandrewwebber) and Facebook (facebook.com/andrewwebberwriter)

Printed in Great Britain
by Amazon